UGLY BETTY

THE BOOK

UGLY

BETTY

THE BOOK

Written by ANN DONAHUE · *Designed by* HEADCASE DESIGN

UGLY BETTY THE BOOK
A BANTAM BOOK 978 0 553 82081 2

First published in Great Britain by Bantam,
an imprint of Random House Children's Books
A Random House Group Company
First published in the US by HYPERION

This edition published 2008

1 3 5 7 9 10 8 6 4 2

Produced by MELCHER MEDIA, 124 West 13th Street, New York, NY 10011 www.melcher.com

Bantam Books are published by Random House Children's Books,
61–63 Uxbridge Road, London W5 5SA

www.kidsatrandomhouse.co.uk
www.rbooks.co.uk

Addresses for companies within The Random House Group Limited can be found
at: www.randomhouse.co.uk/offices.htm

THE RANDOM HOUSE GROUP Limited Reg. No. 954009

A CIP catalogue record for this book is available from the British Library.

Printed in Singapore

This month in MODE

MODE

A MEADE PUBLICATION

THE MASTHEAD

Bradford Meade
CEO, MEADE PUBLICATIONS 1947–2007

Alexis Meade
EDITOR IN CHIEF

Daniel Meade
EDITOR IN CHIEF

CREATIVE DIRECTOR Wilhelmina Slater

EXECUTIVE PRODUCERS
Silvio Horta, Marco Pennette, Jim Hayman, Salma Hayek,
Ben Silverman, and Pepe Tamez

CO-EXECUTIVE PRODUCERS
Bill Wrubel, Tracy Poust, Jon Kinnally, Henry Alonso Myers,
Richard Heus, and Teri Weinberg

SUPERVISING PRODUCER/DIRECTOR: Victor Nelli Jr.
CONSULTING PRODUCERS: Sheila Lawrence and Charles Pratt Jr.
PRODUCER: Dawn DeKeyser
STORY EDITORS: Veronica Becker and Sarah Kucserka
CO-PRODUCERS: Jim Klever-Weis, Shawn Paper, and Jeremy Beim
ASSOCIATE PRODUCERS: Gregg Fishman and Samantha Thomas

ASSISTANT TO DANIEL MEADE: Betty Suarez **ASSISTANT TO ALEXIS MEADE:** Nick Pepper
ASSISTANT TO WILHELMINA SLATER: Marc St. James
KEEPER OF THE CLOSET: Christina McKinney
ACCOUNTANT: Henry Grubstick
RECEPTIONIST: Amanda Tanen (Sommers) **INTERN:** Justin Suarez

---

ADVERTISERS

CEO/FOUNDER OF FABIA COSMETICS Fabia **BEAUMART** Ted LeBeau

IN MEMORIAM

Fey Sommers
EDITOR IN CHIEF

UNKNOWN–2006

MODE

A MEADE PUBLICATION

CONTRIBUTORS

DANIEL MEADE
Co-editor in chief of *Mode*. Charged with: trying and failing to ignore scantily clad models in the morning, in the afternoon, and at night. While he inherited his father's taste for the ladies, he has a humanity to him that the elder Meade lacked.

ALEXIS MEADE
Co-editor in chief of *Mode*. Duties include running faster to the printer than the other co-editor in chief and being able to bench-press more than anyone on staff while wearing a low-cut dress.

WILHELMINA SLATER
Creative director of *Mode*. Among the daily tasks required for this position are plotting, scheming, conniving, calculating, and yelling at models who eat. Loves her job, and woe to those who don't love the idea of her being in charge.

BETTY SUAREZ
Assistant to Daniel Meade. Duties include keeping in line all the lunatics who walk through the front door of Meade Publications and helping unearth the hidden editorial talents of *Mode* co-editor in chief Daniel Meade. Isn't too shabby herself when it comes to putting pen to paper.

MARC ST. JAMES
Assistant to Wilhelmina Slater. Daily tasks include staying three steps ahead of fashion trends while keeping lips firmly located on boss's booty the entire day. Underneath the silk shirts, he has sympathy for kids who are having a bad day. (See Justin Suarez.)

NICK PEPPER
Assistant to Alexis Meade. Charged with: overwrought snarky comments, evil stares, fratty behavior, alienating co-workers, occasional jousting. MBA preferred.

CHRISTINA McKINNEY
Keeper of The Closet. Displays, arrays, and fixes the frays on all the garments received at *Mode* for layouts and photo-shoot consideration. A talented designer in her own right, she's the most popular person on staff when she regularly cleans out The Closet to accommodate new items.

HENRY GRUBSTICK
Accountant. Tasked with seeing through the lies Wilhelmina tells on her expense report and double-, triple-, or quadruple-checking with Betty to make sure her figures are right. Good at math, and actually likes it. Science is exploring this oddity.

AMANDA TANEN (SOMMERS)
Receptionist. Duties include sighing heavily and occasionally answering the phone. There are some skills underneath the prickly exterior, as she did a fine job during the brief time she worked as Daniel's assistant while Betty was at *MYW (Modern Young Woman)*. (And—gasp!—dare we say she has a conscience? She *did* feel bad about selling out Daniel to Wilhelmina as part of an office power play.)

JUSTIN SUAREZ
Super intern Suarez was born to bear the odds and ends of *Mode*—and let's face it, they're mostly odd. From assisting a blind Wilhelmina to moonlighting as a fashion elf to chasing down every minuscule request for Shakira's photo shoot, Justin's savvy in both official and unofficial capacities is endearing and enduring.

CLAIRE MEADE
Widow of Bradford Meade, CEO of Meade Publications, which owns *Mode*. Job requirements include getting off the hook for murdering the previous editor in chief and persevering through decades of marriage to loutish Bradford Meade.

BRADFORD MEADE
Departed head of Meade Publications. Was in charge of making big-budget decisions, including trying to pay off gender-reassigned child with multimillion-dollar checks. A scoundrel, but a rich, respected scoundrel—and on Wall Street, that's golden.

FEY SOMMERS
Not-so-dearly departed editor in chief of *Mode*. Job requirements included minimal calorie intake, love-dungeon maintenance, and daily pedicures. Despite this appallingly overloaded schedule, she still managed to put out an iconic fashion magazine.

CHAPTER ONE

FIR

ST
& FOREMOST

This fairy tale begins, as most of them do, with a young woman. You see, before there was our Betty, there was a Beatriz.

Beatriz Pinzón Solano was the main character in *Yo Soy Betty, la Fea*, a Colombian telenovela that first aired in 1999. Beatriz was bright and ambitious—but a touch lovelorn and a little behind the fashion times, which made her the center of unwanted attention at Ecomoda, the fashion-design company where she worked.

Ben Silverman, now chairman of NBC Entertainment, saw that the tale had promise, and knew that American audiences would love it—hey, we always root for the underdog! His production company, Reveille, and its head of scripted development, Teri Weinberg, teamed with Salma Hayek—no stranger to telenovelas herself—

and her producing partner, Pepe Tamez, to bring the tale to American television.

But these four weren't the only fans of Beatriz in Hollywood. Silvio Horta, the wise and wisecracking executive producer and screenwriter of several TV shows, grew up watching telenovelas with his mom. He joined the team and by writing the *Ugly*

Betty pilot, gave voice to a crazy, kind, campy, heartfelt world.

All fairy tales have obstacles to overcome, and bringing *Ugly Betty* to the screen was no different. What actress could portray Betty, making her both clumsy and lovable and getting audiences to look beyond the bad bangs and the tacky—um, we mean unique—sweater-vests? Here's a hint:

"I was doing an off-Broadway play in New York. Teri and Silvio came out to see me in the play, and then we went to dinner. I was so nervous. I just really wanted it. I just knew."

As it turned out, the producers just knew about America Ferrera, too. Her sweet and sassy take on Betty accomplished exactly what the show demanded: give Betty brains—but also give her a big heart.

This Cinderella story, however, doesn't stop with the belle at the ball—and the TV season doesn't stop with a slam-dunk pilot episode. Over the past two years, a staff of top-notch behind-the-scenes talent was welcomed aboard the *Betty* bandwagon to develop the show further, including executive producer Marco Pennette, executive producer/director Jim Hayman, supervising producer/director Victor Nelli Jr., and co-executive producer Richard Heus. (Who knew that a girl as down-to-earth as Betty would have such an entourage?)

Here is the tale of how the hard work of these folks brings a wonderful, engaging show to your home every week. It's a labor of love for this cast and crew, who are as thrilled as can be to participate in a fairy tale that prominently features a heroine with adult braces. Their work on the show has gone on to win Emmys, but their efforts have also been rewarded by the audience. Just as predicted in the beginning, we've all fallen in love with Betty.

LETTER FROM THE EDITOR

In Hollywood-speak, Silvio Horta and Marco Pennette are known as the "show runners," the people responsible for the creative direction of the show, the ones who agonize over whether Wilhelmina's latest scheme is deliciously bitchy—or just bitchy bitchy.

Silvio, who wrote the pilot, has an office on the second floor of a Spanish-style bungalow on the lot where *Ugly Betty* films in Hollywood. It's spacious, complete with a bathroom and couches, and has a nice view of the surrounding residential neighborhood. But most of the time Silvio doesn't get a chance to take in the view; instead he sits in front of the computer on his desk, or on the couch with his laptop, masterminding the latest adventure for Betty and the gang. After generating buzz by creating both the sci-fi show *The Chronicle* and the cult hit *Jake 2.0* and writing the quip-tastic screenplay for the film *Urban Legend*, Silvio honed his voice—both earnest and snarky—to perfection in the pilot for *Ugly Betty*, which wowed the industry with its combination of charm, wit, and honesty.

Downstairs in the same bungalow, Marco is the ringleader of the writers' room, where the *Ugly Betty* wordsmiths gather to chart out ideas, punch up lines, chew endless sticks of free gum, drink diet soda, and figure out if Henry and Betty will wind up together. Marco has executive produced and written for several series, among them *Caroline in the City*, *Crumbs*, and *What I Like About You*. He brings a fun energy to what could be an incredibly draining process. Words are hard—and funny words are even harder.

And there's another piece to the puzzle of getting *Betty* out the door and onto our TV screens: executive producer and director Jim Hayman. Jim is in the middle of the action, having directed numerous episodes of *Ugly Betty*, including the wrenching back-to-back of "East Side Story"—the first-season finale—and "How Betty Got Her Grieve Back"—the second-season opener. Before joining the *Betty* team, Jim worked on the classics *Northern Exposure* and *Joan of Arcadia*; the latter earned him an Emmy nomination for Outstanding Drama Series.

Together, Silvio, Marco, and Jim keep the *Ugly Betty* train on the tracks, making decisions on everything from casting to music selection to the critical question of whether or not Amanda's prosthetic butt looks too big in a certain scene. Ah, Hollywood glamour!

Below: executive producer and director Jim Hayman and executive producer Silvio Horta.

How Betty Came to Be

Silvio Horta: Ben Silverman—he's now over at NBC—had optioned the rights to the Colombian telenovela, so the project was around for a while before I even came into the picture. There was a sitcom script of it written at NBC five years ago that didn't get picked up, and then it was in development at ABC, and Salma Hayek had come aboard to help produce it. I remember reading about it in the trades and thinking, Oh, that sounds like a cool project! I was working on something else, and I kind of wished I was doing *Ugly Betty*, because I knew the original show. My mom and I would watch all these telenovelas, so I grew up immersed in that telenovela world. *Ugly Betty* sounded like it had the potential to be something that I could nail, that my voice would be good for. And the project I had been working on didn't go through, and we just sort of came together—Ben Silverman, Teri Weinberg, Salma Hayek, Pepe Tamez—we all saw what *Ugly Betty* could be in the same way. I wrote the pilot, Richard Shepard directed it beautifully, and we got picked up.

Marco Pennette: I loved what Silvio created with Betty, the message of "Accept me for who I am; I'm not going to change, and I'm OK with that." It is such a great message to put out there. I did sitcoms in the late '90s, the era of too many skinny girls on television. These young girls at home are watching, saying, "I want to be that!" I remember getting a letter during a show I worked on that said, "I won't let my daughters watch your show anymore. Those women are too skinny." I realized that we do have a responsibility here.

America the Beautiful

Silvio: For the show to progress, it had to be cast contingent. We had to find our Betty. We had America Ferrera in our minds since the beginning, since my first conversation. At the time, I wasn't familiar with her work, and I started watching her movies.

Marco: I watched the pilot when I was interviewing for the job, and I found myself weeping by the end of it because of America. There was a vulnerability there. I'm a big sucker for vulnerability. You know at the end of *Notting Hill* when Julia

Above: executive producer Marco Pennette.

Roberts says, "I'm . . . just a girl. Standing in front of a boy. Asking him to love her." Those are the moments that get me. America just captured my heart, and I thought, Wow, if despite all the craziness that goes on around this show, she can land this every week and ground it, we will have the recipe for success. I went in and said, "I want to do this."

Silvio: It was so clear that there was no other person but America. She was the one.

In the Beginning

Marco: I created a show the year before for ABC that wasn't going forward, so I had the choice of sitting at home with my family and developing a show or working five days a week. (Laughs.) I really was reluctant to do the full-time work, and Silvio said, "Just watch this pilot. We really think you can do this." So I jumped in.

Silvio: We shot the pilot in New York, but we moved to L.A. because it was more affordable to shoot here. And it has worked out in many ways. There's a great group of people, great crews, and a great place to film. There are certainly times when I'll look

at the pilot and those exteriors and think, Oh, I wish we could do that. But CG (computer-generated) technology fixes it well.

Jim Hayman: One of my favorite things about this show—and it started during the very first episode I directed—is that I was often laughing too much to say, "Cut!" So I would snap my fingers when I liked a take. The crew would hear this (snaps fingers), and then I'd start laughing. I'd never been on a show like that before.

Marco: The day production started, my partner and I were having our second child with a surrogate, and she went into labor . . . four weeks early! I called Silvio and I said, "Um, I can't be there. I'm having a baby." He said, "Fine, take the time; don't worry about it." So we had the baby. The next day I woke up with an adult onset of chicken pox. So I called Silvio again and said, "I think you might want to replace me because maybe it's not in the cards for this to happen." And he was great. I'll always save his e-mail, which said, "We will wait for you. I think your voice is important on this show." I sent the writing staff a big basket of cookies with a note saying, "I hope you guys think I'm worth it, but I will be there someday." Two weeks later, I came in.

Jim: I had done *Joan of Arcadia*, and then I was looking around for another job as a director/producer. I was actually very close to taking a job in Vancouver, which would have taken me away from my family here in Los Angeles. Silvio's agent, who is also my agent, said, "Well, you ought to go meet the *Ugly Betty* team. They're thinking about hiring someone in your position." So I had a meeting and—this is really classic Jim Hayman—I called my agent afterward and said, "Forget it. Never gonna happen." And he said, "What are you talking about? They loved you." Now I had to choose between these two shows. Obviously, it was a big draw to stay here. So I sat down with

my family and we looked at both pilots. They looked at *Ugly Betty* and they looked at me and said, "Are you out of your mind? Do it!"

Silvio: We worked so hard and, especially the first few months, it was eat, sleep, work. Like lather, rinse, repeat. I had no life whatsoever. Obviously, I would see the ratings. I saw that we were doing well, and that people liked the show, but I didn't get a sense of this being something really big until the Golden Globes. To get that recognition and to be up onstage? It was just bizarre. Sarah Jessica Parker walked past

and said, "Oh, I love your show!" And I was like, "You watch it? You know the show? You watch the show?" It was so strange. It has been surreal.

The Cast and Crew

Silvio: Vanessa Williams's name had come up earlier during casting, but she was out of town. She was spending time with her family, so we never got a chance to meet. But the casting train keeps on moving, and when Vanessa's name came up again, she was available. She was in New York! Vanessa was really the only one who didn't

audition. And when I was watching the monitors on her first day, I was like, "Oh, God, please!" We struck gold. It has been the luckiest and greatest thing. When Becki Newton came in to audition, we were bawling. We had tears in our eyes. She was just so funny. We shot the pilot in New York, so we did a lot of our casting there. And thank God, because that's where we found Michael Urie and Mark Indelicato. Otherwise, they just wouldn't have been part of the mix. Ana Ortiz came in and was funny, vivacious and strong, and there was also the terrific Tony Plana. I'd written the Christina part initially as a tough-talking

This page, clockwise from top left: Becki Newton (wearing a fat suit) and Michael Urie; Eric Mabius; Becki Newton; America Ferrera.
Opposite page, clockwise from top: Ana Ortiz; Lorraine Toussaint and Judith Light; Vanessa Williams; Mark Indelicato.

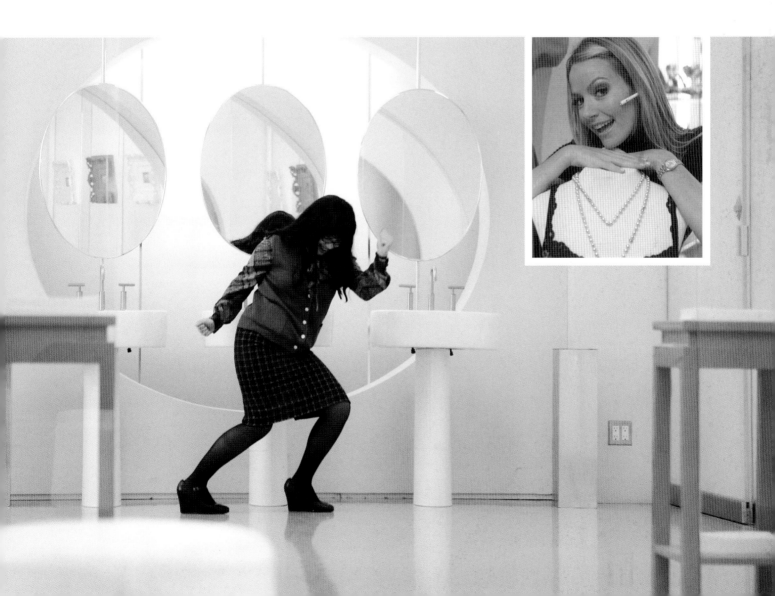

New Yorker, but Ashley Jensen is this Scottish woman who was hysterical and different. Eric Mabius's role as Daniel is difficult. How can you be likable but also a scummy playboy? He had the playboy thing going, but then he had this vulnerability that was really wonderful. It all just came together.

The Day to Day

Silvio: Our job is so big and involves so much that it's a little bit of everything. Getting the scripts perfect is really the most important thing. We have a great staff. We've shifted into more of a sitcom style of writing, where we do a lot of it in groups. We put scripts on an overhead projector and go through them line by line. I've never worked that way.

Marco: We write jokes, and we love all of them. Sometimes we forget that we have to sit right next to the actors as they go over the script at the table read. Once Wilhelmina turned to Alexis and said, "I never noticed what big man hands you have!" We thought it was funny in the writers' room, but there were moments when I'd turn the page of the script and think, Oh my God, I can't watch Vanessa say "man hands" to Rebecca. Once in a while, they'll look at the writer like, "I can't believe you guys are doing that to me!" But they're really great about it.

Silvio: You get better jokes when you do things as a group, and it makes everyone feel invested in the script. It's less lonely, too. You always write a first draft alone, but going through it together is really fun.

Marco: We get funny memos about our scripts from the studios, like, "You're allowed to say four asses and two bitches." And I'm like, "Can I trade you a bitch for an ass?" We do some weird bargaining like that.

Jim: I am responsible for guiding other directors in the basic look and tone of the show and helping them interpret the script. I split time with Silvio in the editing room on all the cuts, and I direct four or five episodes

Opposite page, clockwise from top left: Becki Newton, Michael Urie, and Vanessa Williams; Kevin Alejandro and Jim Hayman; Ana Ortiz and America Ferrera.

WHERE DID *UGLY BETTY* COME FROM?

Ugly Betty is the American version of a telenovela—a Spanish-language soap opera—that first aired in Colombia in 1999. Called *Yo Soy Betty, La Fea*, it starred Ana Maria Orozco as Beatriz—nicknamed Betty—who worked at a fashion house called Ecomoda. (Sound familiar?) She's the assistant to the new president of the company, Armando Mendoza, and her workspace is a storage room in the back of his office. On her first day of work, she orders coffee to be delivered and has to clarify, "I am Betty . . . the ugly one," to make sure it is brought to the right person. So sad! But little do the folks at Ecomoda know that this ugly Betty graduated with degrees in economics and finance—with honors, mind you—speaks multiple languages, and could pretty much run the place with one hand tied behind her back.

Now, we all know that's a setup rich for great television—and the rest of the world thinks so, too! There are versions of the Betty story in at least ten countries, ranging from Mexico's *La Fea Más Bella* (which stars Angélica Vale, whom you may recognize as the orthodontist's reception-ist from *Ugly Betty*'s first season finale) to Israel's *Esti Ha'mechoret*, which translates to "Ugly Esti."

a year. I direct the season opener and the season finale, and two in the middle that I try to span out to keep a sense of continuity with the actors. We also have another incredible director/supervising producer, Victor Nelli Jr., who directs episodes. A one-hour drama is funny in that you don't have two or three directors who do everything, which at the end of the day would probably be the best thing for the actors, because there's a certain level of trust that has to be won. I think my job as a director is creating what I call "the bubble"—a sense of safety and security that allows the actors to do their work. Familiarity is a big part of that, but directing every episode is just too much damn work! (Laughs.)

With Special Guest Star . . .

Silvio: It's so rare that a movie-star producer on a show actually wants to be a part of it. Salma was great and she was game. We were so happy. It's really a testament to her love of the show and her commitment to it. We wrote the part of Daniel's love interest Sofia Reyes and she said, "You know, I think I want to do it. I think I want to try it." She was excited and just jumped in there. She knew the arc and that at the end she was going to be this villainess. She relished it.

Marco: We did an episode where Rebecca Gayheart played Alex Meade's ex-girlfriend. She and Rebecca Romijn kissed each other

good-bye. Now, I guess I should feel as though progress comes in baby steps, because I remember when Roseanne kissed Mariel Hemingway fifteen years ago: it was earth-shattering. We didn't get a note from the network about our show's kiss. But I did discover that they wouldn't use it in the promos because it's an eight o'clock show. At first, the hair on the back of my neck went up, but then I thought, You know what? Five years from now, that won't be an issue. We are moving forward.

Silvio: Lucy Liu told me she was a fan of the show, and we said, "We have a part!" We had this attorney character who was sort of a love interest for Eric. We thought it could be really fun for her.

Marco: We tried to get Taye Diggs for an episode last year. He was all set to do it, but then he got a big hit spinoff [*Private Practice*]. I still see him at the events for ABC, and he always says, "I'm so sorry that didn't work out." I love him for that and hopefully we can get him to do an episode if he's not too busy. Audra MacDonald's joining him on the show. I'm circling that cast for guest stars! [*Private Practice* and *Ugly Betty* film on the same lot.]

Silvio: Marco is a big, big musical-theater fan and was completely over the moon about Patti LuPone. I had been a fan of her work for a while and had a conversation with her on the phone once about a pilot I

was doing. The role of Marc's mom came up, and it was a no-brainer.

Marco: Patti LuPone told a story while we were rehearsing. She did the scene where she disowned Marc. Marc told her he was gay, and she basically said, "If that's your life, you're dead to me," and walked out of the room. We were all there watching it, and Jim Hayman and I were crying. She turned and said, "Do you want me to cry?" And I said, "I don't know." She later said that a director told her, "If you cry and the audience cries, that's good. If you don't cry, but the audience cries, that is better. But if you cry and the audience doesn't cry, that's bad." I thought that was great.

The Best of *Betty*

Silvio: There's no one—whether they're pretty or ugly or skinny or fat or rich or poor—who cannot relate to this girl. There's nobody who hasn't felt like an underdog at some point in their lives. Everybody has at some point felt like the outsider. Betty is this optimistic girl we all aspire to be.

Marco: I never bought into that "You're changing the world with your half-hour sit-com" thing, but now I do see it with *Ugly Betty* a lot.

Jim: The thing I like most about Betty is that she gives hope and inspiration. She is undaunted in her attempts to find truth.

Silvio: She is a moral person who does what we all wish we would do under some of the difficult circumstances she finds herself in. But she's not a pushover. She's strong and has a very specific point of view on what's right and wrong. She's valiant.

Top: America Ferrera.
Bottom: Gina Gershon and Vanessa Williams.

SPECIAL GUEST STARS

She's too humble to admit it, but Betty is a hit in Hollywood! Check out just a few of the stars who have taken a turn on the show—either playing a role or appearing as themselves:

1 **GINA GERSHON** as Euro-fabulous advertiser Fabia • 2 **SALMA HAYEK** as Daniel's love interest Sofia Reyes 3 **FREDDY RODRIGUEZ** as Gio, the ambitious sandwich maker • 4 **LUCY LIU** as legal eagle Grace Chin • 5 **JERRY O'CONNELL** as fratty bar boy Joel • 6 **PATTI LUPONE** as Marc's mother, Mrs. Jean Weiner • 7 **RITA MORENO** as Ignacio's sister, Mirta • 8 **KRISTIN CHENOWETH** as the orthodontist's assistant, Diane • 9 **ANGÉLICA VALE** as the orthodontist's receptionist (Vale plays protagonist Leti on *La Fea Más Bella*, the Mexican version of *Ugly Betty!*) • 10 **VICTOR GARBER** as Betty's writing teacher, Professor Barrett • 11 **JAMES VAN DER BEEK** as sleazy fashion head Luke Carnes • 12 **VICTORIA BECKHAM** as herself • 13 **MARLO THOMAS** as magazine advertiser Elaine Winthrop • 14 **TIM GUNN** as a Fashion TV correspondent • 15 **VERA WANG** as herself • 16 **ILLEANA DOUGLAS** as Sheila, *Mode's* new creative director

CHAPTER TWO

FAM

ILY

FOUND: in the "tube" hallway at *Mode*. The materials placed along the sides of the halls change every episode. Wilhelmina will not tolerate wilting! This jarred fruit gives a splash of color to the white, white world: "If it's too stark white, it's not in keeping with the tone of the comedy and the sort of comic-book world that this show can be," production designer Mark Worthington says.

TRUE PASSION

FOUND: in the Suarez kitchen. It's a modest plant. But it's real! And it needs nurturing! Which makes it, of course, a perfect metaphor for Betty in the hyperplastic space of *Mode*. "We usually come up with a whole backstory for a character," Mark Worthington says. "When you're really doing your job, the design will suggest the décor."

Despite being fashion-backward,

Betty Suarez

is the kind of woman who

never goes out of style.

The heart of the Suarez clan—and perhaps the only person at *Mode* to even have that organ—she eventually wins everyone over with her innate dignity, noble spirit, generous nature, and ability to stand up for herself and those she loves. (True, she hasn't won over Wilhelmina yet. But give her time.)

"When was the last time a young, female-centered show wasn't about what she looked like or her sex appeal?"
—America Ferrera

Betty has certainly captured the imagination of those who dreamed her up in the first place—the cast and crew of *Ugly Betty* are effusive when they talk about the character. She earns plaudits for her resilience at work: "Betty is a winner, first and foremost," says Brian Tanen, the assistant to executive producer Silvio Horta. "Everyone is skinny and perfect and beautiful, and she comes in with a look that is the opposite of what is expected of her, and she triumphs." Others say that Betty's love life is lovely to behold: "Betty is just not your normal romantic heroine," says story editor Veronica Becker. "She's not Cameron Diaz. She's not Drew Barrymore. And to see a girl like that fall in love with a guy who is her match, and not with JFK Jr., is

a really nice wish fulfillment to give to all the girls out there." And finally, her home life: "She is defined by her capacity to love," says Tony Plana, who portrays Ignacio. "She cares about everything, everybody, whether they hate her or not. It's an amazing virtue."

And there's nothing more satisfying than seeing all these attributes in action on screen. Let's not forget how she responded to one of Marc and Amanda's original catty ploys, the nonexistent Halloween contest: "Hey, where's your costume? What about your e-mail yesterday about the *Mode* costume contest . . . which . . . was . . . obviously sent only to me. Well, then. I guess I win!" Yes, Betty, you always do, and that's what makes you so great.

Let's set a few things straight: America Ferrera has perfect teeth—no need for braces here at all. She doesn't wear glasses—the pair in the show belongs to Patricia Field, who designed the costumes for the pilot. The one thing that's all America is her talent: after a stunning debut in HBO's 2002 movie *Real Women Have Curves*, she found a perfect fit in *The Sisterhood of the Traveling Pants* films. But it is the character of Betty Suarez that shot her to superstardom—the Dorothy who, in a whirlwind, is sucked from her comfortable home to become a stranger in the strange land of high-fashion publishing.

A Conversation with America Ferrera

From Beauty to Betty: It takes about forty-five minutes for the Bettyfication—an hour, tops. I just have to pull on the wig. A lot of it is in the braces—and the braces take half a second because they're a retainer. I got away with a lot of anonymity at first because people knew the character and not me. But then we did a lot of press, then came the awards, and now it's pretty insane. I spend a lot of time at work and I don't spend a lot of time out in the real world, so I have no idea what's really going on out there. One of the first times I had a break, I went to New York City and got stopped every ten feet: "You're Betty! You're Betty! You're Betty!"

Heart and Soul: I love coming to work and not having to worry about what I look like. It's just such a freeing role. What I love about Betty is that all her vanity is gone, giving me a wide-open space to dig into

America Ferrera was the producer's dream choice for the role of Betty. Opposite, top: America without her Betty hair, glasses, and makeup. Opposite, bottom: Shooting a scene. This page: Rodman Flender directs the now-famous Halloween epsiode.

the heart and soul of the character. She has an endlessly optimistic energy, and that's fun to play.

Salma the Saleswoman: Salma Hayek came to me a year before the pilot was even made, in January 2005. She explained the character to me and the premise of the show, and I just immediately fell in love with them. I don't know if it was who she is or how enthusiastically and wonderfully Salma explained it—she's got the ability to sell anybody a used car. (Laughs.) I felt like the character and story were lacking in the entertainment industry or at least lacking in the television landscape. When was the last time a young, female-centered show wasn't about what she looked like or her sex appeal? And what really got me was when Salma said that Betty was smart. She's really smart, and she's really caring and loving. She brings out the good in other people, and I thought, Wow, what a wonderful superhero.

Getting the Role: In January 2006 it was: "We're going to do it! Here's a script! And

we've got the director! We've got it all! It's on!" I was doing an off-Broadway play in New York. Two of the producers, Teri Weinberg, who's now at NBC, and Silvio Horta came to see me in the play and then we went to dinner. I was so nervous. I just really wanted it. I had to do a screen test, so they sent a director to New York, and he directed some of the audition scenes on the set of *Hope and Faith* in Queens. I didn't Betty myself up for it—I just did it as my real self. I figured that they would imagine the rest. It was really nerve-racking for about a week, and then I got the phone call! We shot the pilot for fourteen days in March.

I Heart New York: The pilot was shot in New York, which was amazing. We shot in the Woolworth Building and Times Square—it was gorgeous. The city was a part of the show. After filming, you sit around and cross your fingers and hope that it happens. And then we got picked up, but we were put in a really weird time slot: Friday at 8 p.m. Then they changed the name of our show from *Ugly Betty* to *Betty the Ugly*. And it was all just wrong. (Laughs.) But I had faith that it would all happen the way it was supposed to. When the critics got a glimpse of the show and wrote all these wonderful things about it, we got moved to Thurs-

days and then they gave us our name back, *Ugly Betty*. And so then all was as it should be.

Hair-raising: My real hair was used in the pilot, except for the hideous bangs. That was not my hair. I felt that if I'm going to play this character for the next seven years or however long, I wanted to feel a little different in my own life. So literally the day after we wrapped, I started threatening the producers that I was going to go shave my head. I've always wanted to shave my head. And they kept begging me not to do it. They'd say, "America, no!" And then one day I was walking down the street and felt so sick of my hair, so I had it chopped to my chin. When they saw me with my short hair, they wanted to kill me. Thus, we have the wig, which is so much better, because for me, at least, it's like I put Betty on and I'm Betty, and then I can take her off and walk away.

Fan-tastic: If I wasn't a part of the show, it would be on my TiVo list. It's a show that I would love. The most exciting part for me is to get the script and find out what's going to happen. I'm a fan. I think the writers are great. I thought the first season finale was amazingly put together. I get very emotional at the table reads, and that scene with Ana was really hard to do. I love Betty and

Betty's Glasses

Betty's most defining accessory might just be her glasses! Not quite cat's-eye coy, but not desperately dorky, either, Betty's red specs set her apart, frame her face, and show that she has a sense of fun. For a character who gets relentlessly teased about her fashion sense, there's a bit of irony in the source of Betty's glasses: they originally belonged to Patricia Field. (Fashionistas fawn over Field, given her credits on *Sex and the City* and *The Devil Wears Prada*.) The woman has an eye to die for—and, apparently, the glasses that covered those eyes were the perfect fit, as well. After America Ferrera tried on countless pairs that weren't quite right, Field handed over her own glasses—and Betty's look (quite literally) was born.

Henry. I'm a big romantic-comedy sap girl. Whenever they write cute romantic things for Betty and Henry I get really excited because that's what I love to watch. And so it's fun to play them.

It *is* a Small World, After All: At the Halloween parade in West Hollywood, there were so many people dressed up as Betty. That was when we realized we might have something here. And because the show represents almost every kind of minority you can think of, there is a wide audience. There are a lot of different groups of people who find positive representation in the show.

Bumps and Bruises: I get hurt all the time. I'm just a very clumsy person. I read Lucille Ball's biography, and she was always in the hospital for dislocated knees and ankles, so I guess it's like anything for a laugh, right? As long as it's funny.

First Awards Show: We were on the air for six episodes and got nominated for a Golden Globe. I was much more focused on whether the show was going to be good. Were people going to watch it? I just wasn't thinking about the awards, not so early on. So when we won, it was an amazing surprise. We got a lot of love from the critics and we got a lot of love from the viewers. We're only in our second season, so it's insane.

Life on Set: We have this incredible, incredible cast. Not only is everyone so talented, but we all love one another. We really enjoy being around one another. The crew is amazing—they feel like family. We're proud of everything that happens and that we've created this wonderful little world.

No Apologies: What's great about the show is that it's fun and entertaining, but it's also like taking medicine with a spoonful of sugar. You learn something from the morals and the goodness and the feelings, but you didn't realize that you learned it because you were too busy laughing. We can address a lot of really hard issues with humor. And what's wonderful about all these characters is that no one's apologetic about who they are. They're just who they are, and they embrace it, and they love it. Even Wilhelmina—she is not sorry for being a bitch. Marc is by no means ashamed of who he is. He thinks he's wonderful. And Amanda thinks she's wonderful. And Hilda thinks she's wonderful. There's an overwhelming amount of narcissism on our show, so it doesn't matter how much you bash the characters—it doesn't faze them. (Laughs.) They love themselves! And so it's really a show full of Bettys—people who just accept who they are and run with it. I think it's a change to see characters who don't pity themselves or don't victimize themselves, you know?

GET CAUGHT:
Sleeping!

Betty:
Hilda, I know what the *curandera* meant! The tree is the family tree. And the missing branches—that's Mom's side of the family. It's, like, so obvious. She wants me to fill in Mom's side of the tree.

Hilda:
Well, you could climb it with those toenails.

Betty's goal in Guadalajara: To fill out her mother's side of the Suarez family tree. For this and other lofty goals, it's wise to get a good night's sleep. Head gear optional.

BETTY'S LOVE TRIANGLE, U

Betty is probably the last girl on Earth to think she has a complicated love life. But when you put it down on paper, it is a tangled little web. (But not in a depressing *Charlotte's Web* kind of way. Although if it was like *Charlotte's Web*, "GO FOR IT, HENRY" might be written in big letters.)

MARC
But just for the sake of his mother's visit

DR. GABRIEL FARKAS
One disastrous date with Betty led to him meeting Charlie, which led to serious baby-daddy drama over who was the father of Charlie's baby. Those racheros! *Enfuego!*

BETTY
Our Heroine!

CHARLIE
In a parallel universe—where Charlie wasn't Henry's ex from Tucson and didn't get knocked up and didn't cause a world of hurt, confusion, and literal tug-of-war over who the father of the baby was—she and Betty would totally be friends.

HENRY
People, Betty and Henry aren't Geek—they're Greek. As in tragedy. One's available, the other's not. Henry wasn't sure if he was the father of his ex-girlfriend's baby. Betty doesn't really have problems like that. But are sympathized? Star-crossed lovers? Absolutely!

GIO
Under all that antagonism, could sandwich man Gio really be carrying a torch for Betty? After all, Henry is going back to Tucson.

GINA GAMBARRO
If she keeps at it, Queens is going to be renamed Trampsyl-vania. She's too busy making out on her couch with someone new every single night to watch her replacement plasma TV.

WALTER
He was Betty's first love, but the pressures of Mode and his opportunity to manage a Pro Buy in Maryland drove them apart—not to mention his entire dalliance with Gina Gambarro. Besides, who really wants to date someone who knows how long it takes to digest corn?

DANIEL
Why is Daniel on this list? Pipe down, all you people on the internet who constantly post about such things! Okay, sure—in most of the international versions of Ugly Betty, she winds up with her boss—but stateside they're just friends for the foreseeable future.

THE WOMEN OF MANHATTAN, AND POSSIBLY OTHER BOROUGHS
See page 73, Seaf Player. Immediate disqualification for Betty.

HILDA
It's hard to be the center of attention when you've got a sister like Hilda. She and Daniel shared a drunken kiss at Fashion Week, and she and Gio went dancing together.

Hilda Suarez

After getting used to Hilda's big hair, big nails, and big attitude, seeing Ana Ortiz in person can be a bit of a shock. She's refreshingly lovely, with a model's perfect cheekbones, a giddy grin, and none of the brassiness that is her character's stock in trade. After years working in New York theater, Ana was on a roll, with roles on high-profile TV shows, including Steven Bochco's war tale *Over There* and the acclaimed *Boston Legal*. But it's in the role of Hilda that Ana really shines, since there's nothing like playing a character who loves to be the center of attention. And Ana's home life is just as fulfilling: she married musician Noah Lebenzon during the summer between filming the first and second seasons of *Ugly Betty*.

A Conversation with Ana Ortiz

The Suarez Clan: I think we're Betty's support system. We're her cheerleading squad, and when she has moments of self-doubt, we're there to show her that she's more than capable. We're behind her, no matter what happens. When I was young, I assumed things would just fall into place for me. But you graduate from college and then life knocks you over, and it's difficult not to think, "Poor me" and "How am I going to make it through this?" Betty is going through that. Here is somebody so young who continues to face life with a smile and a positive attitude. It's good to know that no matter what, she's still got a crew behind her that's going to be there through thick and thin. It makes it a lot easier to face these really difficult situations.

Lil' Sis: My favorite quality in Betty is her resilience and also her complete conviction in herself. She knows that that she can accomplish anything she sets her mind to. When she gets knocked over, she just pops right back up with a smile on her face. She definitely has some attitude. I think she gets that from her family. (Laughs.)

From Playing Betty to Playing Hilda: My agent called me before the script was even written and said, "There's this project that Salma Hayek is producing. It's called *Ugly Betty*. It's based on a soap opera. This is it. This is the one. I just know it. I can just feel it. You've got this. We've got to get you in on it." And so they sent me out to audition for the role of Betty. I was like, "Y'all, this is not right." They were like, "Just get really ugly and wear lots of layers and just go in there." And I replied, "This is not my part. It's too young. It's just . . . it's not . . . this is wrong." And they said, "Just go in anyway. They want to see you." So I went in and obviously was completely wrong for the part. But that being said, you have to look at any audition as an opportunity to do your thing, so I did the best I could, and they called me back for the role of Hilda.

Hilda 1.0: When I first auditioned, the script had Hilda with little Justin and pregnant

"I look at some of these costumes and say, 'You guys, there is country-music big hair and then there is Queens big hair, and never the twain shall meet.'"

with another. She was married, not living in the house, and was also shopping for a minivan. She was totally different than the character she is right now. Five auditions later, the character had been rewritten and became what she is now. It was really exciting to see the evolution of that, even in the audition process. That has never happened to me before, so it was very cool.

Hilda's Evolution: I remember going in for my audition and thinking, Well, she's selling Herbalux, so what is a Queens woman's idea of a professional look? I knew she was just a fiery Latina, so I thought, I'm from New York, she's from New York; I'll just copy all of my cousins.

It's Got the Look: The show itself is just so beautiful to look at sometimes. There's so much color. It's like America always says—

it's eye candy. Everything pops. Even in our crazy little Queens house with all the newspapers and the craziness, there's still all this vibrancy. There's always somewhere for your eye to go and something to look at that's interesting and beautiful.

Queens Style: Getting to look like Hilda takes about two to two-and-a-half hours, depending on her look for the week. I look at some of these costumes and say, "You guys, there is country-music big hair and then there is Queens big hair, and never the twain shall meet." I think it's such a perfect fit for Hilda to be at beauty school. It just makes sense because our show is so hair-intensive. Our hair-and-makeup department is just beyond brilliant and so helpful about showing me how it's done.

Crying on Cue: When I got the script for the season finale, I thought, Oh my God, how am I going to pull this off? It's always difficult for me as an actress to have a sudden burst of emotion. In theater it's a lot easier because you have the buildup of the entire show to get you where you need to be emotionally. Doing a television show or movie, it's like, roll the cameras, action, cry! I was genuinely worried I wouldn't be able to do justice to such a beautifully written and beautifully shot scene. And in the second-season opener, there was more mourning. I was really, really lucky that the way they wrote it had Santos being brought back in Hilda's imagination. I had this wonderful actor, Kevin Alejandro, with me. He couldn't be more supportive. It counts so much to have a connection with the person you're in the scene with. The people who are casting our show are so brilliant. I'm finding that those scenes that I'm so worried about often come quite easily because I'm working in such a supportive, incredible atmosphere. I was really lucky to have Kevin come back and help me with that. The fact that it truly was his last episode with us was enough to make me weep. Weep that he's going to be gone, that my little Justin's not going to have a dad. I was really able to put myself into the reality of the show.

Ana Ortiz showed stunning range when she took high-maintenance Hilda into a dark place after the death of Santos. Opposite page, top: Ana in the Suarez house set. Bottom: As vibrant Hilda. Below: Kevin Alejandro's nuanced performance showed Santos's development from cad to family man.

Hilda's

In a rush? Stayed out too late? Had to climb up the drainpipe in the morning to get back in the house and now you need to get ready superfast in order to take your kid to school? Hilda Suarez gives you tips on how to apply your makeup perfectly in fifteen minutes.

Now, we all know that we have inner beauty, but sometimes it takes a couple of tricks in the morning to make that shine through, right, girls? Here are my five secrets to looking great when you got lots of bad happening and little time to make it good:

1 Preparation H under the eyes. Yes, I know what it's meant to be used for—get your father to buy it for you at the drugstore and no one will look twice. Slap it on when you first wake up and then—this is VERY IMPORTANT—be sure to wipe it off before you leave the house. Shrinks those bags right up!

2 Pick a brighter shade of blush than you usually use. If you're tired, your skin is going to be sallow, and a fresh shade of fuchsia or tangerine will really pick you up. And ignore that nonsense that you may read in beauty magazines about applying blush only to the apples of your cheeks. Just go for it. All over. No one knows where the apples of their cheeks are, anyway.

3 Coffee.

4 This is really hard for me to say, but when time is critical, you have to forgo the false eyelashes. I know that for many people a day's look isn't complete without them, but if you're in a hurry, this kind of sacrifice must be made. Instead, apply several coats of two different formulas of mascara—one made for lengthening and another developed for thickening.

5 Lip liner, lip liner, lip liner. It helps your lipstick stay in place, and if you've applied your favorite shade of Caribbean Kumquat in a hurry, there's a high chance you look like the crazy lady at the bodega who never buys anything but is always in there petting the cat.

So there you have it! Oh, wait! You wanted hair to be included in the fifteen minutes? No way. That is impossible. Give me another half hour, or an hour, tops, and I can do hair. But fifteen minutes? No. Unless you're Gina Gambarro and don't have any shame about running out the door with your cheap rat's nest of a weave half falling out. Then fifteen minutes is totally doable.

After

GET CAUGHT:

Spraying!

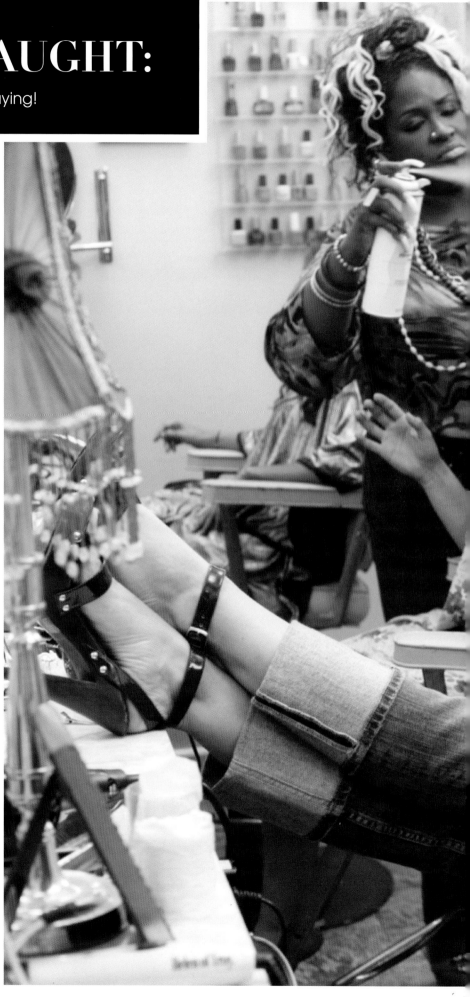

"Betty, you want to fit in with these people? I've got news for you. They're not going to change. You have to."

—Hilda

Always looking out for her little sister, Hilda helps Betty get a makeover to fit in with the fashionistas at Mode. One little problem—Hilda's Queens hot still isn't midtown Manhattan hot.

Justin Suarez

Out of character, Mark Indelicato looks like your typical Los Angeles thirteen-year-old: he wears aviator sunglasses, loves to play his Nintendo Wii, and has a burgeoning interest in fancy kicks. After hitting all the right notes in musical theater in his hometown of Philadelphia, Mark found his first long-term TV role in *Ugly Betty*, and he has already cemented his reputation as a scene stealer with his complete, total fantasticness. Mark moved out to Los Angeles with his mom, Lynn, when he got the role of Justin—and was thrilled that, after a year away from his family, his father made the move to the West Coast for the filming of the second season.

A Conversation with Mark Indelicato

Not Your Typical Kid: Justin is this fashion-forward awesome kid who doesn't care what other people think. He just goes out and does what he loves to do. He's not the typical kid that you would find on the streets every day. He's more complex than that. He's a unique person. That's why I love playing him so much. He's not the jock—he shines in a way that nobody else does. I feel so blessed and honored to be playing such a wonderful, different character that no one has ever seen on television before.

Little Music Man: I started in theater—yeah, the singing didn't come out of nowhere. (Laughs.) I worked my way up from there. My favorite song from the show would have to be "Good Morning, Baltimore." That was

superfun—dancing around on the subway. I actually went to the premiere of the movie *Hairspray*. Oh, my God. It was so much fun. John Travolta was so funny. All of the actors played their characters really well. I couldn't stop laughing the whole time.

Getting the Role: I auditioned in New York. My manager found out about the audition and I went on that, like normal. Then I went through all of these callbacks. Then I finally tested with America and got the pilot, so here I am!

Happy Feet: Sometimes I'll trip and fall or stumble on the words or forget the dance move. We mess up a lot. (Laughs.) At least I do. And you know, when you mess up, you just laugh and start over and keep rolling. I don't mess up too much. I study my lines. It's just that sometimes when you're doing

the scene, you stumble on the words and we laugh and have to start over.

Bigger and Better: Day-to-day life has been different over the past year because the show has gotten bigger and bigger and our characters have gotten bigger and bigger. Going to the mall isn't the same anymore.

School Daze: I'm in an online charter school that is funded by the state of California. They send you a computer and books, and I have a teacher who does all the work with me. So it's like going to school—except you don't have to go to school. I like it. Since the show's gotten popular, it's kind of hard for me to go to school. A lot of schools frown on kids getting out early, and why pay for a private school when I'm never going to be there?

GET CAUGHT:

Reenacting your favorite musical theater in the subway!

"Idea! I'll catch you up. Let me set the scene: Baltimore, 1962. The height of segregation and the beginning of the teeny-bop revolution. Our heroine's Tracy Turnblad. Chubby but totally adorable. She wakes up and begins to sing . . ."

—Justin

So what if the only thing Justin knows about the Yankees are that pinstripes are divine? By sharing his passion for *Hairspray* with Santos on the subway, father and son come to an understanding that talent doesn't just apply to playing sports.

Queens, NY

LA FAMILIA

Guadalajara, Mexico

THE SUAREZ FAMILY TREE

While visiting family in Mexico, Betty learned from a wise *curandera* (healer) that she needed to examine her family tree.

HILDA (translating): She says you're stuck . . . You can't move forward until you look back. But there's hope. She sees a tree.

BETTY: A tree?

HILDA: With branches missing . . . the answer's behind it.

BETTY: What does that mean?

HILDA: It means the woman's nuts. A minute ago she was eating a candle.

FIRST GENERATION:

YOLANDA:
Rosa's mother, Betty and Hilda's grandmother, Justin's great-grandmother, Ignacio's mother-in-law
"If you love someone, you must find a way to be with him. Even if you have to leave your family."

SECOND GENERATION:

IGNACIO SUAREZ:
Betty and Hilda's father, Justin's grandfather, Rosa's husband
"I remember the first time your mother made me dinner. It tasted like shoe leather, but I didn't care, because she made it."

AUNT MIRTA:
Ignacio's older sister, Clara's mother-in-law, Betty and Hilda's aunt
"Why shouldn't I cry? I haven't seen my little brother in thirty years. I want to say you look the same, but you look like an old man. And that means I'm old, too."

ROSA SUAREZ (RIP):
Betty and Hilda's mother, Justin's grandmother, Ignacio's wife, Ramiro's ex-wife, Yolanda's daughter

RAMIRO VASQUEZ:
Rosa's abusive first husband, whom Ignacio presumed he killed in a fight (but actually didn't!).

THIRD GENERATION:

BETTY SUAREZ:
Ignacio and Rosa's daughter, Hilda's sister, Justin's aunt
"Before my mom died, she told me the most important thing in life is to find someone who loves you. And when you do, hang on to them no matter what. Because in the end, that's all that really matters."

HILDA SUAREZ:
Ignacio and Rosa's daughter, Betty's sister, Justin's mother
"The test said I had to do a manicure. It didn't say on who. I wasn't gonna waste this hotness on somebody else."

SANTOS (RIP):
Hilda's fiancé, Justin's father
"Yo, you got something to say? Digame, chico. Now, my son's gonna keep telling me about the Hairspray, OK? And when he's done, you better clap."

CLARA:
Betty and Hilda's cousin, Aunt Mirta's daughter-in-law
"Enough with the beans and cheese. You want to order Chinese?"

FOURTH GENERATION:

JUSTIN SUAREZ:
Betty's nephew, Hilda and Santos's son, Ignacio's grandson
"It's women-in-history week and I'm doing an oral report on Nicole Richie. I think she's just at the beginning of her importance."

Ignacio Suarez

We've become so accustomed to seeing Tony as the generous, thoughtful Ignacio that watching him in other roles—whether portraying a terrorist who plots dastardly deeds (in *24*) or in uniform as a military man (in *An Officer and a Gentleman*)—is jarring. It's a testament to his skill, which has been honed through decades of work on stage, TV, and the big screen. (Yes, that's him, playing Jefe opposite Chevy Chase, Steve Martin, and Martin Short in 1986's *Three Amigos*.) Friends say the role of Ignacio is closest to who Tony is in real life: earnest, soft-spoken, and deeply attached to his family.

A Conversation with Tony Plana

"Te Quiero": There are so many lines that are my favorites. This is going to sound corny, but I'm the dad, so I can afford to be corny. I think my favorite expression on the show was "Te quiero": I love you. I started saying it in the last episode of the first season when I'm in Mexico. We're separated, and at the end of our phone call, I say, "Te quiero" to Betty, and in the first episode of the second season, she says it back to me. I think it's an important line because it shows that we need to tell each other that we love each other. We cannot take it for granted, because I think love needs to be a practice. It cannot be assumed. It needs to be practiced every day and needs to be expressed every day through actions and through words; otherwise, you lose it.

Top Chef: I think that Ignacio is one of those fathers who is deeply identified with the family, and defined by it. His life is about the family, for the family. And his cooking is the way that he loves his family, nurtures them, takes care of them, and nourishes them. It is where he's an artist. He's a chef—at least he used to be. He hasn't been able to express that, but I'm hoping in the future that talent can be expanded. But it's all tied in to the family. One of the things they miss most when I'm away in Mexico is the cooking—there's nothing to eat! Justin is starving, you know? I love the fact that it speaks to the narrowness of defining Latino men stereotypically. There's a feminine side to cooking that he has adopted. I like that he is very comfortable with it.

Theater Experience: I think the nature of the show requires that actors are theatrical in their background. It also requires actors who are capable of doing both drama and comedy. I've been fortunate enough to have been hired for both.

Class Conflict: I'm most proud of the show for not being a fluffy comedy or some sort of fluffy satire. It's rooted in substantive issues that are relevant to everyday life: feminine image, self-image, economic and social limitations or barriers or stereotyping. I love the contrast between the dysfunction of the Meades, which is endemic to affluence, and the dysfunction of the Suarezes, which is endemic to working-class realities: health issues, legal issues, immigration issues, employment issues. Look at Hilda, the daughter who hasn't gone to college, and then Betty, the daughter who has. It's the wonderful message that if you go to college, you have more options.

Celebrating Justin: I wasn't sure where Ignacio stood at the beginning. He was worried about Justin, and when Santos is negative toward the boy, he's forced to take sides with the mother against the dad's position. That's a seismic shift for Ignacio. He says, "Hey, where do I stand here? I stand with this boy. I love him as he is, unconditionally, forever. I don't care what happens or who he is or what he does. I love him and I'm here for him." I've always had difficulty with the narrow definition of Justin as gay or pre-gay or potentially gay—all that stuff to me is insignificant. He is a budding, blossoming artist who is highly sensitive and has an incredible eye and ear for art, music, and design. And it's all about nurturing that, helping develop that, and validating it every day. I like the fact that in our show, those barriers between sexes and gender are blurred.

Access Your Style | MAKE

Make your kitchen a cozy
spot with color and kitsch.

OVER YOUR HOME

Use framed photographs and meaningful pieces to make your home a haven.

THE SUAREZ HOME

CHAPTER THREE

CAR

EER

V

FOUND: in the *Mode* closet, with other ideas that didn't work out. "The chain-mail babies were pretty great, I have to say," laughs Mark Worthington, *Ugly Betty*'s production designer. When Daniel called in too hungover to work, Betty was forced to deal with the photo shoot for celebrity baby Chutney—and the appalling idea that Chutney should be wired up in chain mail and drenched in water. Edgy! Also, wrong! But great!

TRUE PASSION

FOUND: on Betty's desk, until it was stolen and tortured. A slightly corny but seriously sweet representation of Betty's supportive home life, the bunny Hilda gave her when she graduated from Queens College has been through a lot at *Mode*—just like Betty. Yes, Marc and Amanda tortured it, but in the end, the bunny prevails. "You need to get into the head of the characters to determine what is going to support the scene in a literal way," Worthington says.

TEN RULES
EVERY ASSISTANT SHOULD KNOW

We've seen Betty learn from the school of hard knocks at *Mode*—and while she has held up quite well under the strain, not everyone would be as resolute in sticking with the gig. Did you just get hired as an assistant? We're so sorr . . . happy for you! Happy! Here are some tips to make your life easier:

1 Don't answer the phone if you have a mouthful of food. There's nothing more embarrassing than the person on the other end hearing something completely unprofesh when what was actually said is "Daniel Meade's office, this is Betty."

2 Always be suspicious when the craven, manipulative harpy in your office starts being nice to you.

3 Know what kind of bagel your boss likes and how much cream cheese. Know the second choice of bagel as well, and never listen when he tells you he wants an onion bagel on the day of a big meeting.

4 Keep the company's FedEx shipping number hidden on your desk; otherwise certain other people in the office (they might be named Marc and Amanda) might start selling their swag on eBay and shipping it on the company's dime.

5 Be sure to wear comfortable shoes to the office, in case you have to run. People may rag on your sensible footwear, but when they have to chase a transgender glamazon to the printer, they'll be jealous.

6 Set up a Google News alert on sweatshop labor and eradicate any offending clothing or accessories from your boss's wardrobe.

7 No matter how hot the weather is, or how much the air conditioning in the building is being stolen by the piggy guys at the sports publications on the other floors, do not wear shorts to work. Because you will be mocked.

8 Order twice as many office supplies as you think your boss needs. There might be occasions when your sister visits your workplace and steals the extras. Or your nephew, during his internship, might go on an origami-swan Post-it note binge.

9 When ordering the champagne for the office Christmas party, it is perhaps not the best idea to have the office lush sign for the delivery.

10 Floss after every meal, every snack, every last jelly bean stolen from the communal jar. Food getting stuck in your braces and then meeting the boss's clients? Not so cute.

Lowlights

The Top Ten Most Ridiculous Office Tasks Assigned to Betty

10 Fronting the cash for Daniel's morning bagel when he was short. Who's the millionaire scion here, anyway?

9 Driving to New Jersey to pick up a pimped-out wheelchair for Daniel . . . when Daniel could walk all along.

8 Buying a "plastic thingie" so Daniel's office chair doesn't get caught up on the carpet. Princess? Meet the pea.

7 Calling Tiffany to order "the usual" for one of Daniel's lady friends. Buy stock in Tiffany!

6 Being forced to take the stairs with Daniel for twenty-eight floors to the *Mode* offices so he could avoid running into Sofia in the elevator. There's cardio, and then there's crappio.

5 Having to track down reindeer—or, failing that, goats—for the Christmas photo shoot. Next year? Herding cats.

4 Being asked to leave Thanksgiving dinner with her family to help Daniel pick out what shirt to wear. What a turkey.

3 Chasing down Daniel's Days of the Week girls in order to find his watch. Monday's child was fair of face, but she was kind of a bitch, anyway.

2 Picking the cabbage out of Daniel's coleslaw. Which leaves mayonnaise and carrots.

1 Standing in for a Brazilian model in Phillippe's photo shoot. Yep, this is the one that made Betty quit—but it's also the task that made Daniel realize how valuable she is as an employee. All's well that ends well—at least until Daniel makes Betty pay for his bagel again.

HOW TO
Deal with Criticism at Work

Betty is made of stronger stuff than most of us. Despite working at *Mode*—where mean girls go after they grow up and fail to marry rich in college—she has figured out how to respond appropriately to all the flak that gets flung her way on any given work day. What lessons in resilience can we learn from Betty?

Ignore

Hey, everybody has a bad day. Sometimes little snippy comments are going to be directed at you, and these are the times to roll with the punches. Check out what Betty has put in the back of her mind:

Betty: *I know most of your magazines inside out. I try to devour as much as I can.*
HR Guy: *Clearly.*

Wilhelmina: *She's cleaning The Closet tomorrow. Christina needs to make room for the spring collections coming in. Freebie couture is the staff perk. Bustiers, lingerie, hot pants. You really should take a trip down there, Betty. There might be some . . . socks in your size.*

Respond

Constructive criticism should serve as an opening to engage in a worthwhile discussion! There might be little pangs to your feelings, but don't take it personally. Such comments will ideally lead to a rational conversation between adults. Right, Betty? Right?

Betty: *Maybe your concept of what's beautiful is a little narrow!*
Bruno: *Excuse me?*
Betty: *If you can't find the pure wonder and joy in a baby, and think it's edgy to drown her in chain mail—*
Bruno: *I've been styling for this magazine, hon, since before you bought your first pair of orthopedic pumps.*
Betty: *Yes, and for the record, your "brilliant" cover of Courtney Love leaving rehab in a wheelbarrow of pills was our lowest-selling issue in seventeen years. Maybe you're not the right person for the job.*

Daniel: *I'm so sorry. I was a jerk. I really messed up. I didn't mean those things I said. I need you in my life.*
Betty: *Good. 'Cause when you hired me, you got more than an assistant; you got a friend. That's just who I am, Daniel. When you screw up, I'm going to be in your face whether you like it or not.*
Daniel: *Good! Yes! That's what I want. So, are we OK?*

Quit

Screw 'em. They suck. Get out of there. Did you know Starbucks has benefits for part-time workers? As Betty knows, wearing a hat that doubles as a tortilla-chip tray is far less humiliating than dealing with a liar.

Betty: *You manipulated me. You lied to my face about Daniel.*
Sofia: *I did. But I never lied about you. About your potential. Your abilities. That's why I hired you. Because I see so much of myself in you.*
Betty: *Well, I don't see any of myself in you. Here's my article about working at Mode. Funny thing researching it—those people may be superficial, but they know it. And they don't pretend to be anything more than they are. And I actually think I fit in better there than I ever will here.*

GET CAUGHT:

Learning!

"And if there are no old wounds, well, as I always say: 'If you have nothing to write, try killing yourself. If you fail, you'll have something to write about. If you succeed, your troubles will be over.'"

—Professor Barrett

Betty attempts to prove that she's a writer, dammit, not just an assistant, by enrolling in imposing Professor Barrett's writing class. After panicking and passing off another woman's story as her own, Betty learns that beauty is truth, truth beauty.

Can Your Boss Be Your Friend?

Daniel Meade

Daniel Meade loves the ladies, the ladies love him, and he loves to be loved by the ladies. This has landed him in a heap of trouble—everything from legal scares to drug addiction—but Daniel is kept in check by the ever-vigilant Betty, who has become a friend as well as his assistant. Daniel's hold on the top job at *Mode* is precarious, as he always has to fend off Wilhelmina as well as other interlopers who aspire to head the company (hi, Alexis!). But underneath the pretty-boy exterior, Daniel wants to be as great a leader as his father was—except maybe he'll handle all the lady business a little better. He has already managed to be a professional who professes to care about his workers—and follows up when it matters most. (Betty thought she'd never have a chance to fly on an airplane—let alone fly first class to Mexico, thanks to Daniel!)

"(Daniel and Betty) end up really doing much better together than they would separately."—Eric Mabius

One of the most commonly asked questions to insiders on the *Ugly Betty* set: "Is Eric Mabius as hot in person?" Well, uh, yes. But don't hate him because he's beautiful. Eric gave a stunning debut performance playing an aspiring rock star in 1995's Sundance hit *Welcome to the Dollhouse*. Since then, he has received acclaim for his performances on *The O.C.* and *The L Word*. And playing cheeky Daniel gives Eric a chance to act out—in real life, he's happily married with a toddler.

A Conversation with Eric Mabius

A Very Betty Honeymoon: They were looking to cast the role of Daniel, but I was out of town because I was getting married in our home down in New Orleans. My agent and my manager kept bothering me, saying that I needed to come back because there was this project called *Ugly Betty*. And I said, "There's no way I'm coming back." I was going to go on a honeymoon! But I have some persuasive people working with me, so the day after the wedding, I ended up flying back and meeting with them. I read the script when I was in New Orleans, and I thought, Wow, this is great, but it's probably going to fail miserably because it's brilliant on the page. Generally what happens is, if something's really good on the page, it ends up getting watered down. It just doesn't work out in the end because there are so many cooks in the kitchen. But

I went and met with them. I thought they were going to cast some actor who can play an obvious ass. Someone who's a little more spot-on. I thought, They're not going to cast me in a role like this. But they said, "No, no, we really want you." And then they brought me in in front of the executives at ABC Studios, and they cast me right away.

Sophomore Success: There's something unbelievable about the writing staff. I think the second season clicked even better than the first in ways that we couldn't have possibly anticipated. We were totally blown away by the second season, which is good because of that little fear that creeps in after such a strong first season, like, Oh, it couldn't possibly be as good as the first. Often the people on the writing staff of a show are just trying to find themselves in the first season, not excelling the way that ours have. It's amazing.

The Right Tone: We never do things in a sappy way. The humor makes the drama land and vice versa. To that end, I think the writing is fairly realistic even though it's cast in a sort of over-the-top, campy world. There are some very real lessons going on; you don't learn something automatically or change a person immediately. It takes months and years to implement the lessons that we learn. There are some really touching scenes with Justin that I like. We get more of that in the second season.

Brotherly Love: Well, I think they sort of intentionally softened me for that story line to get me ready for [the appearance of Alexis]. But it's a great prize to find out that you have a dead brother who's now your sister and she's going to be played by Rebecca Romijn. It could be worse.

Eric Mabius on set in Hollywood. (The New York skyline behind him is a fake. Hollywood magic!)

MY·W

A MEADE PUBLICATION

FROM
FLING
TO
RING
IN
60
DAYS
>It's Easier Than You
Think (Pg. 48)

INVEST >
THE
BEST
WEB
TOOLS
TO
MANAGE
YOUR
NEST
EGG

FEBRUARY 2007
ISSUE 1 • VOLUME 1

$7.99 US $8.99 CAN £3.50 GB

0 74470 02051 6

02>

PREMIERE ISSUE!

"Silvio really sets Daniel and Betty up as parallels: similar people, but from entirely different backgrounds, both in over their heads."
—Eric Mabius

Opposite: The premiere issue of *MYW (Modern Young Woman)*, Sofia Reyes's magazine.
Below: Daniel Meade commits another fashion don't while on office grounds.

The Best of Betty: I think Betty's indomitable spirit is obvious to everyone. It's infectious to everyone who watches the show and the characters in Betty's world, but I also think that there's a more subtle thing going on. She chooses to stay the way she is in spite of being totally cognizant of the mocking she receives and the people who are constantly trying to cut her off at the knees. She still maintains that spirit with the full knowledge that she is different. There is an easier way, but she chooses not to go in that direction. Her spirit ends up rubbing off on everyone around her. No matter where we're from or what we do, we all want to fit in. But she chooses the tougher road.

Perfect Pair: Silvio [Horta, executive producer] really sets Daniel and Betty up as parallels: similar people, but from entirely different backgrounds, both in over their heads. And then they sort of complete each other in an odd way. Silvio keeps having them be similarly challenged in each episode. In the first season, Daniel was having affairs of the heart and learning how to have adult relationships, and at the same time, you'd see Betty trying to do the same thing, trying to struggle through her relationships with Walter and Henry. I see them as indivisible aspects of each other. They're the unlikeliest of partners, but they end up doing much better together than they would separately.

Life Lessons: Daniel has not been given the necessary basic tools to get through the challenges he faces. Yet he still manages to get by, in large part because of Betty's influence and the upbringing she has had and the love she has for her family. She rubs off on Daniel quite a bit. Granted, for every lesson he learns, he takes one step forward and ten steps back.

Good to Be Bad: I've never played a character like Daniel. I think back to the shows I watched when I was growing up, like *M*A*S*H*. In the earlier half of its run, the character played by Alan Alda was just the most delicious. He's vulnerable, he's sympathetic, but he's also a rogue and could be an obstinate bastard if he chose to be. Daniel is not totally dissimilar from that. He is the heroic antihero.

THE MEADE FAMILY TREE

Sometimes, the Root of the Problem Is Family

It is nature, but not quite natural.

BRADFORD MEADE (RIP)
What a tangled web you wove, Bradford.

CLAIRE MEADE
Bradford's widow; mother to his
two adult children.

WILHELMINA SLATER
Bradford's fiancée, whom he left
on the altar by, well, dying.

FEY SOMMERS (RIP)
Bradford's longtime lover.

ALEX/ALEXIS MEADE
Bradford and Claire's oldest daughter,
who was their son but underwent gender
reassignment surgery, which s/he
forgot about after a car accident.

AMANDA TANEN (SOMMERS)
Fey's daughter and NO RELATION
TO DANIEL. NOT AT ALL.
Because that would be dirty.

DANIEL MEADE
Youngest son of Bradford and Claire who
still hasn't forgiven them for that—
there's nothing like having to live up to the
perfect big brother. Big sister. Whatever.

HALSTON
Fey's dog; Amanda's adopted
canine sibling.

LOVE TO LOVE YA, BABY!

Take our quiz to determine which *Ugly Betty* character's love-life your love-life most closely resembles!

1. Your dream romantic vacation is:
A. One season at the Four Seasons.
B. Tucson, Arizona.
C. Dude cruise—ahem—we mean a Caribbean cruise.
D. Paris in spring—no, wait. Paris in fall—no, wait. Paris in summer. Winter sucks, even in Paris.
E. Anywhere his private jet flies.

2. Your new significant other is dropping by in five minutes. You hide:
A. My other significant other.
B. Hilda.
C. My Kylie Minogue nesting dolls.
D. Halston.
E. Anything not cashmere or fur.

3. Your ideal mate drives:
A. Red stiletto heels.
B. A Prius.
C. A stick shift.
D. Something with a big backseat.
E. Just one car? Absurd.

4. Your idea of a perfect first date is:
A. Somewhere the paparazzi won't find us.
B. Dinner and a movie.
C. Breakfast at Tiffany's, lunch at Barney's, dinner at his place.
D. Breakfast at Tiffany's, lunch at Barney's, dinner at his place.
E. Snuggling after a State of the Union black-tie function.

5. The sexiest food is:
A. Breakfast in bed.
B. French fries.
C. Slightly seared Kobe beef.
D. A prix-fixe menu.
E. Caviar.

If your answers are mostly:
A. You're a Daniel. You put lust at the top of your list.
B. You're a Betty. You'd love to be in love, but life keeps getting in the way.
C. You're a Marc. Your waters run shallow, but that end of the pool is the most fun.
D. You're an Amanda. You go for what you want, but deep down you yearn for some stability.
E. You're a Wilhelmina. Your power is to attract those who are more powerful than you.

DANIEL'S MANY CONQUESTS
(in Manhattan and possibly other boroughs)

{1} Charmaine: Good at dictation.

{2} Amanda: Thankfully, they're not related.

"Red Turkey": Betty had to babe-watch this one outside Daniel's apartment.

Friday: No watch here!

Thursday: No watch here, either!

{3} Sofia Reyes: Brutal *bruja*.

Lara: Sofia's assistant with the Tiffany necklace.

Aerin: Awww, Daniel's first supermodel.

{4} Grace Chin: From not to hot.

Petra: Not sixteen, but still rock bottom.

Marla: Allergic to pants but likes *Hotel Rwanda*.

Sandra Winthrop: Some would call her a cougar, but that would be catty.

{1}

{2}

{3}

{4}

GET CAUGHT:
Working!

"Meade Publications
has always been
owned and controlled
by a Meade. And
when Alex died, that
pretty much left me
as the heir apparent—
not exactly what my
father was hoping
or expecting."
—Daniel

Shoved into a high-powered work position
he didn't feel entirely ready for, Daniel
dedicated himself to regaining his father's
confidence by making *Mode* as perfect as
possible.

Dealing with a Diva!
Wilhelmina

Fine, so she's not editor in chief of *Mode* (yet). But she may play an even more important role in the *Ugly Betty* universe. Combine *The Wizard of Oz* with *The Lion, the Witch, and the Wardrobe*, and what do you get? The Wicked Witch of the Wardrobe. That's precisely Wilhelmina. Despite facing hardship (who else is deposed by a back-from-the-dead gender-reassigned heir and has her fiancé die on the altar?), Willie bounces back with another plot, another scheme, another path to the top. And that's why we love her.

Let's take a quick look at Vanessa Williams's résumé, shall we? She's an Emmy-, multiple Grammy-, and Tony-nominated performer, with more than one million albums sold. You would assume that with those credentials, in person she'd be, shall we say, Wilhelmina-like? Far from it. Warm and down-to-earth, Vanessa is about as far from a diva as you can imagine. (Can you picture Wil happily boasting about sending her oldest child off to college in the fall?) And now, after all her success, Vanessa has found a home on *Ugly Betty* that allows her to showcase her theatrical training, her singing (it was Vanessa's voice singing while Wil was imagining all of her good memories of Marc in Season One), and her love of getting the laugh.

A Conversation with Vanessa Williams

Welcome Aboard: The producers came to me the night before they were about to shoot the pilot and told my agents, "Listen, she's our first choice." I was living in New York, so I just showed up. Patricia Field, who did the costumes for the pilot, called me that night and said, "Bring anything in ivory, everything in ivory!" So I brought all my ivory stuff and met her in the wardrobe trailer that day. My first scene was the one where I'm in bed with the French photographer. I'm wearing a bra and I'm under the covers, like, "Hi, guys!" Then I finished doing the shooting and had to leave to sing at Katie Couric's colon cancer benefit at the Waldorf. It was a very busy day, to say the least.

The Plane Truth: I would travel back and forth between New York and Los Angeles every weekend, so I would always go through the metal detector, and that's where I'd get my feedback from people about Wilhelmina. There are no streets to walk on out here, and everyone's in the business anyway, so you don't really get to meet fans. Traveling, however, is a good way to get a sense of who's watching and paying attention. Flight attendants like us!

Witch Way?: I've got to hand it to Silvio for creating Wilhelmina—she was so clear on the page that it's just really easy to execute her. Sometimes I wonder, How did they know I would play this so well? But then I thought back: I've played a witch in *Into the Woods* on Broadway, I've done the *Diva's Christmas Carol* for VH1, and even in *Kiss of the Spider Woman* I was a diva. So I said, "OK, now I see that they know I have the breadth to do it." It's always great as an actor to have the confidence of knowing that they think you can pull it off. They give me the material, and I run with it.

Babes in Arms: If you were trying to be transformed into the most beautiful thing ever, Rebecca Romijn is who you want to be. She's such a good sport. You have to be able to make fun of yourself on this show, and she does it all the time. When we had that scene where we're back to back in the mirror, people were like, "Oh, my God! I can't wait to see what's going to happen!"

The Beauty of Betty: I think that Betty is very likable to people from a wide range of ages and backgrounds. She's truly a fighter and a modern woman, and though she might be a little challenged in coordinating her styles, she's courageous. She's the Norma Rae of young twenties, and it's great to be able to see that every week on TV.

Slater

"Sometimes I wonder, How did they know I would play this so well?"

—Vanessa Williams

Not on Autopilot: Richard Shepard, who directed the pilot [and won an Emmy for his work], was genius. He gave *Ugly Betty* its look—that clean, contemporary, well-shot look that is beautifully lit. It made the show stand out and look more like a feature film than your average television show. I saw his film *The Matador* on one of my flights back and forth to New York, and I definitely could see his style and why they went after him. The camera's always moving, so there's always a sense of anticipation. But it's very stylized, too.

The Big Apple: When we moved to L.A., we just had to surrender to the process. Most of us were living in New York when we got this show, and we thought, Wouldn't it be great if we got employed in New York? Here was a television series that might actually shoot in New York! That was the big appeal. Once that changed, then the concern was that the set was never going to look like New York. How are we going to live up to the pilot, which was spectacular? With the magic of special effects and greenscreen, they do a

Hey, we thought white was supposed to represent innocence. Wilhelmina guards The Book, right, and treats herself to the best as she prepares for a night out with The Senator, below.

"This is one of those shows where the director can say, 'Bigger!' That freedom as an actor makes you want to come to work, because you can be large and big and broad, which I usually only get a chance to do onstage."

fantastic job faking out the audience as we shoot in L.A.

Eager Ensemble: We all get along—and that's unusual. (Laughs.) We're not all the same race and age, which is also good. I think it really helps that we're all from such diverse backgrounds. For some of us, this is our fifth TV series, and for others, this is a new experience. We're enjoying the fact that we're working together as an ensemble and it's not just the grind, which it could easily be.

Christmas Gift: In "Fey's Sleigh Ride," my favorite moment was the line, "Did you just gesture at me when you said 'Kwanzaa'?" (Laughs.) It was so strong that I used it as my holiday slogan for my Christmas gifts to the cast and crew. I put it on the side of a mug with a caricature of Wilhelmina.

Going for It: This is one of those shows where the director can say, "Bigger!" That freedom as an actor makes you want to come to work, because you can be large and big and broad, which I usually only get a chance to do onstage.

Wilhelmina Who?: I live in my hometown of New York, where my friends are raising kids, and they don't get a chance to see what I do because they're living their own lives. So the comfort for me is that this is my job, and then I have my family life, and the two don't overlap. I have some friends who are fans, and I've brought their kids on set, and, you know, then I'm the popular neighbor. (Laughs.) But most of my friends say, "How's the show going? Great. When are you coming back home?" You know, "How's camp going with the kids?" I have a great balance.

"I am hellaciously upset, Marc."

on Daniel:

"Oh, my God, this couldn't be easier if I actually gave him the gun and aimed it at his foot."

to Marc:

"Do you know how many curly haired, effete sycophants there are just waiting to replace you?"

on Betty:

"It looks as if Queens threw up."

to Betty:

"You surprise me, Betty. Stealing keys, breaking into my apartment, taking The Book. Good for you. You're growing."

on feeling for Amanda:

"Even if I wanted to express sympathy, I physically couldn't."

on the underprivileged:

"Poor people are so cheap."

on Daniel:

"Look at them falling over themselves to get a quote— as if he actually knew a thing about fashion. The man saw Vera Wang's spring line and gave her a high-five."

to foreign cabdriver:

"It's pathetic. This city hands out licenses to anyone. 'What did you drive in the old country? A goat? Here, have a cab!'"

on marriage:

"Come on, people. Let's get this over with. I mean, let's get me married off to the most wonderful man in the world!"

on the Meade family coming together:

"I hate that love won out."

on her marriage to Bradford:

"Marc, I've got flower problems, catering problems, and Bradford wants something called a Shania Twain to perform at the reception. I have bigger issues now. Find out what Betty's getting for lunch and order me two."

on Alexis:

"Well, I knew a bribe was never going to work with Alexis. She's lonely. Little Orphan Tranny needs a man."

to Betty:

"Betty, dear pie-eyed, pie-eating Betty—his sister lost her memory. He's still in a wheelchair. I know he pays you for your South-of-the-Border spirit, but let's give Daniel a break."

on Betty:

"I don't like it when she smiles. It's so metallic."

BEAUTY IS ONLY SKIN DEEP

...and isn't that fabulous?

Wilhelmina's always ready and willing to try the most avant-garde beauty treatments— with mixed results. Thankfully, her pain is our gain:

Eating is for the weak, right, Wilhelmina? And yet it's amazing how she fails to realize that not eating makes you weak, as well. Wil starves herself to fit into a spectacular dress after Fashion TV mocks her for robbing the cradle.

Marc procures some teeny fish that nibble off the dead skin on Wilhelmina's feet to give her the perfect pedicure. It works, and she hooks foot fetishist Bradford. And Betty thought sushi was gross.

Wrinkles imply concern. And concern implies age. And age implies wrinkles. Fortunately, Wilhelmina breaks this vicious cycle thanks to in-office Botox injections from Marc. And the lucky fella gets to keep the leftovers!

Two words: duck sauce. Oh, Fabia, how could you be so cruel?

From skinny Minnie to maxi-padded, Wilhelmina loses too much weight on the cayenne-pepper-and-lemon-juice cleanse, and her wedding dress looks like a tent on her. For the rest of the week, she orders two of whatever Betty eats to fill it out again.

WILHELMINA'S OFFICE AT *MODE* MAGAZINE

"The white, which I love, took a little bit of convincing because people were afraid of what it would look like on film," says production designer Mark Worthington. "But we kept it and introduced the poppy accent colors." The white also serves to mark it as the domain of the ice queen herself, Wilhelmina. Take, for instance, Willie's chaise lounge in her office, where she receives her visitors and her Botox. "The way it's framed, it's so prominent and really stylish," Mark says. "It's minimal, and yet it's this thing that ultimately expresses her fashion attitude and her power. Instead of a little table with chairs around it where she has meetings, it's her chaise. It's all about her." Most satisfying to Mark, however, is how the modern look of the office, with its splashes of orange and green, inspire the actors and writers to respond to the environment onscreen. When Hilda comes to *Mode* in the first season and says it looks like "gay Star Trek"? Comic—and production design—gold.

Access Your Style **|** DRESS

CHOOSE SLEEK COLORS TO MAKE
OFFICE SUPPLIES AN OFFICE SURPRISE!

DIVA UP YOUR OFFICE AND MAKE YOUR SPACE WORK FOR YOU!

Use white as your accent color. It says, "pristine," "high maintenance," and "do not even think of drinking that cup of coffee in here."

Work Your Way Up!
Marc St. James

Every bad guy needs a wingman, a *consigliere*, a, shall we say, assistant. Marc St. James helps Wilhelmina on her path to the top, be it by procuring skin-eating fish to nibble on her toes for the perfect pedicure or acting as her "seeing-eye gay" during Fashion Week. But he's not just evil doing based on the whims of Wil—Marc can also get his bitch on with BFF Amanda. Getting paid to be at work is one thing, but getting paid to be a jerk is fabulous.

Michael Urie will tell you right up front that it's not easy playing a flying monkey. He's done Shakespeare across the country with ease, produced stage shows, and graduated from Juilliard as the recipient of the prestigious John Houseman Award for ability in classical theater. No problem, right? But playing Wilhelmina's minion Marc requires long hours, insane attention to hair and wardrobe, and constant cattiness. Which is why Michael loves every second of it. Sweet and contemplative in real life, he relishes the chance to bring out his claws every week for *Ugly Betty*.

A Conversation with Michael Urie

Friendly, But Not Friends: Betty wins everyone's heart and then they go back to normal. She won Amanda's heart and then Amanda went back to normal. She won Marc's heart and then Marc went back to normal. It wouldn't be fun if we were suddenly friends. One of the key elements in the episode where she and I bonded and she pretended to be Marc's girlfriend was that at the end, I say, "It doesn't mean I like you."

Rock Solid: I was in New York doing a play and I saw this breakdown for a costar role—a one-line description—Wilhelmina's bitchy gay assistant. I was like, "Hey, I could do that!" So I told my manager to get me in on it and he did. But the play I was doing at the time was about Mount St. Helens, and I played a geologist. And as we all know, geologists all have beards, so I had this big, bushy beard. (Laughs.) I went in, and Silvio liked me, but they wanted me to shave my beard. I was like, "You've got to be kidding.

I've been growing this thing for four weeks. This is my art and you're sacrificing the artistic integrity of the play. I'm really going to have to think about this. . . . I'll do it." (Laughs.) I have to thank Vanessa Williams, because she kept including me in bits and jokes—she kept saying, "Why don't we do this here?" or "What do you think we should do here?" She kept throwing in "Marc!" They ended up keeping all of my stuff, and when we finished shooting the pilot, they put me in the cast photo.

On the Marc: I think that Marc is like many ambitious gay men in fashion. He's pretty much trying to emulate Wilhelmina at every turn until he can be her. I don't know that he has any ambition to do anything but serve her, unless he can take her over and be her instead. He loves her and he loves his job. Probably the biggest similarity between me and Marc is that we love our jobs. If I draw on anything, it's that giddiness to be at work. I have no sense of fashion. I mean, I do have more of a sense of fashion now, but I've learned it from Marc. A year and a half ago, you'd see me wearing a black belt with brown shoes. I would never do that now.

To Be or Not to Be Crazy Busy: I was doing a series of Shakespeare plays in San Diego, every night a different play. Then someone from *Ugly Betty* called and said, "They're picking up the show and they want you to be in every episode!" So for a month, I was driving back and forth. I shot one day until 3 p.m. here, and I got into San Diego at 7:30. Four and a half hours. The show's at eight. It gave me just enough time to get into my wig and my doublet and hose for *Othello*. My understudy was not happy.

THE GRAPEVINE

Quote it, quip it, let it rip. Relive the greatest exchanges between Wilhelmina and Marc, the Queen of Mean and the Queen who has only been to Queens three times—and they were all by accident, he swears.

Marc: I thought breast cancer was pink.
Wilhelmina: It is, but Alzheimer's went better with the dress. What, I'm supporting! That's what counts.

Wilhelmina: Old. Way too old. Marc, I think this one's face is on our money.
Marc: You wanted men who would make you look young.
Wilhelmina: How about finding me one that doesn't leak?

Wilhelmina: I have six hours to become ten years younger and five pounds lighter. What is that?
Marc: A salad.
Wilhelmina: Take it away.
Marc: You have to eat.
Wilhelmina: Whose side are you on? Get out!

Wilhelmina: Back off, girlfriends! Stop pawin' my piece, 'less you gonna show me benjies, know what I'm sayin'?
Marc: OK, L'il Kim, visiting hours are over.

Marc: Good morning, sunshine. I bought you a present. Whole wheat.
Wilhelmina: Too late. Yesterday was carb day.

Marc: Are those blue jeans?
Wilhelmina: Aren't they fabulous? Ted took me to an outlet mall. I shopped next to fat people.

Marc: By the way, when you move into Daniel's office, I am not sitting in Betty's old chair. This bum don't slum.
Wilhelmina: That's not what I heard.

Marc: So I just got an e-mail that Daniel called a staff meeting for eleven. Why does he still get to do that? I thought we were in power now.
Wilhelmina: Relax, Evita. All in due time.

Marc: It's a blessing, Willie! Fashion Week! Think of all the people you don't want to see.
Wilhelmina: But they have to see me. And you'll be by my side at all times. You'll be my seeing-eye gay.

Marc: Oh, thank God, you have a new plan! We shall overcome!
Wilhelmina: You're not allowed to say that.

Marc: Whoa. Fill my bucket with nothing but thighs!
Wilhelmina: Relax, Colonel. We all know you prefer nuggets.

Wilhelmina: He patted my hand.
Marc: Maybe that's foreplay.
Wilhelmina: In a nursing home!

Marc: Will you be back in time for that luncheon for the homeless children?
Wilhelmina: If I'm not, make sure they get their free hair products. Priorities, Marc.

Marc: Little glitch. A teeny, tiny, Cindy Crawford mole-sized problem. It seems St. Patrick's is already booked for June sixteenth.
Wilhelmina: What?!
Marc: Oh, what do you get with St. Patrick's? Bad incense and a lot of guilty men in dresses.

HOW NOT TO SUCK AT SUCKING UP

Not all of us can be as diligent as Marc and de-cob baby corn for our idol/employer. If you haven't had the chance to sleep your way to the top—yet—there are some simple rules to follow to get on your boss's good side:

Do

✳ Know her dietary foibles, such as Tuesday is carb day.

✳ Set a timer on your desk that will remind you to tell your boss how devastatingly beautiful she looks every hour on the hour. (But don't make eye contact when you do this; it might throw you off your game. Kinda like Medusa.)

✳ Grease the wheels of your desk chair to prevent any insonorous squeaks from reaching her pristine ears.

✳ Rip out the size-four tags from the samples designers send over for her and sew in size-two tags.

✳ Add a zero to any "receipt" on her expense report.

Don't

✳ Mimic the way she dresses.

✳ Refer to any actress over the age of twenty-five as "aging gracefully."

✳ Acknowledge the existence of any meddling offspring.

✳ Show her any unflattering paparazzi photographs. That old saw that all publicity is good publicity? Painfully, patently false.

✳ Hesitate even for a second at whatever outlandish, soul-crushing thing she may force you to do.

GET CAUGHT:

In the wrong part of town!

"OK. So. Let's regroup, call another cab, and see if they'll come to Dante's Seventh Circle of Hell. Give me your phone. Willie? Where's your bag?!"

—Marc

Trying to intercept Baby Chutney's arrival at JFK, Wilhelmina mouths off to a cabdriver and gets abandoned in a not-so-savory part of town with Marc. Thank God the church-donation box for the poor accepts diamonds.

Frenemy or BFF:
How Much Can You Trust Your Colleagues?

Amanda Tanen (Sommers)

Oh, the indignities Amanda Tanen must face. First off, she's the receptionist at *Mode*. She's freakin' Fey Sommers's daughter, and she's still just the receptionist at *Mode*. Second, she can't get a guy to commit—although this may have something to do with the fact that she only dates guys who are fully unsuitable and insist on hiding their relationship. Finally, there's the candy-snarfing thing, which, while an efficient stress reliever, only results in endless additional hours at the gym and less time for plotting capers with best friend Marc. But Amanda, with attitude to spare, rises above all these traumas and lives on to torment Betty and get mountains of *Mode* swag.

After small parts in a number of TV shows, Becki Newton hit center stage on *Ugly Betty* and could not be a more deserving subject for the spotlight. There are two things Becki has in common with Amanda: they're both hilarious—and not just the quick-laugh-and-smile kind of hilarious. She's the tears-rolling-down-your-cheeks, catch-your-breath hilarious. (Don't believe it? Check out Becki's commentary track on the *Ugly Betty* DVD.) And yes, she's mind-meld best pals with Michael Urie in real life. In the first episode the duo shot together, she suggested Amanda and Marc strut through the halls of *Mode* arm in arm—and it's been nothing but laughs ever since.

A Conversation with Becki Newton

Revenge on the Mean Girls: I read the script, I guess about a year and a half ago now, and I loved it immediately. I said out loud to my husband, "I absolutely have to get a part on this show." In particular, the part of Amanda jumped out at me because she reminded me of all the girls in my life who have ever been mean to me. I thought, Wow, wouldn't it be fun to actually play one of those girls? The next step was actually auditioning. It was the scene when Betty first walks into *Mode* and Amanda says, "Oh. My. God." And it

What Do You Do with Unrequited Love?

Why isn't the man in your life getting with the program? You love yourself, so why can't he love you, too? Taking lessons from Amanda's relationship with Daniel, the answer is simple: you must kick that hopeless loser to the curb and at the same time desperately, desperately try to make him realize how incredibly fantastic you are.

1　Tell him, to his face, that you don't care about him at all except in a professional/friendly manner. Men always want what they can't have. And then, when he starts dating other women, mimic their dress and styling habits as closely as possible.

2　Drop hints about how incredibly busy you are. Events, galas, functions, parties—so many to attend! So little time! (But don't mention that you're just really busy stalking him with your gay best friend.)

3　Dress like a hooch.

And that's it! If this fails, head to your adopted parents' house in the suburbs, make them go to their nearest giant-mega-discount-mart-store-club-thing and buy a gallon tub of Goldfish crackers, and then hole yourself up in your childhood bedroom for a weekend and cry while watching *Pretty Woman*. Not that Amanda would do this.

made me laugh so much just to practice it that I had to try hard not to make myself laugh during the audition. Because that's kind of obnoxious. (Laughs.)

The Bold and the Beautiful: I got such a kick out of Amanda, and I remember walking out of the audition feeling like it went pretty well. But I wasn't sure if my take on Amanda was the right one because I knew it was quite a take. And then I went back and auditioned again and met Silvio and Salma. Within a week, I had the part.

Snarf!: I really enjoyed Amanda's eating last season. I thought that was hysterical. From one point of view, Amanda's this girl who dresses perfectly. Her hair's perfect, everything's perfect. But the flip side is that she's a total hot mess who binges on food any time she gets a little nervous. From the beginning, the writers made sure they showed the messy side of these seemingly perfect characters. Marc starts wheezing when he gets uncomfortable. I think it's genius.

Mamanda: I love working with Michael Urie. I think that the Marc-Amanda relationship—and I've been told that people refer to it as Mamanda—was great from early on. In the pilot episode, we linked arms and said some nasty lines. From then on, there was a certain bond that the two of us had. Our characters and the two of us as people have a very similar sense of humor. I love how that relationship has developed over the course of the first season and definitely into the second season.

Pals with Michael: There was a phase when Michael thought it was funny to pretend he was getting sick right before they said "Action!" So he would say things to me like, "Did you try that bean dip out at craft services?" And he'd have a look on his face like he was about to throw up and they'd say "Action!" and I'd have to say a serious line. (Laughs.) So that was interesting, the feigning-sickness phase. It was the kind of thing where you don't even realize that something's funny—and actually nothing is funny—but you just start laughing because you're not allowed to.

MARC AND AMANDA, *MODE'S* BONNIE AND CLYDE

You vote! What are the greatest moments in their office alliance?

a The Thanksgiving weekend when they broke into Wilhelmina's office, snarfed up the food from all her gift bags, sang "Dreamgirls" in her couture dresses, and snooped through her phone records.

b The discovery of Fey's love dungeon.

c Marc corralling the paparazzi when Amanda wears red to the Black and White Ball—and unveiling her naughty bits to ensure tabloid glory.

d In-ing the straight-but-pretending-to-be-gay "faux-mo" Tavares at his meeting with Wilhelmina and the buyers.

e Getting the "it" item—the faux-rabbit-fur micro-mini—for Eternal 18 at Fashion Week.

HALSTON SOMMERS

The cutest ugly dog on the catwalk, Halston is provided for hand-somely by Fey's willing of a weekly stipend to cover his care after her death. Thinking that the dog was a cash cow, Amanda was delighted to take care of her dead mom's Chinese Crested—until she learned the horrifying cost of mange medicine.

"Maggie (Halston) doesn't have to do anything, and she's a comic genius. If there's a camera on (her) face, everyone starts laughing."
—Becki Newton

Too Close for Comfort: I like that everyone's mean to Betty and she treats them with the utmost respect. She never holds anything against anyone else. Amanda will rip her apart, make fun of her to her face, tell her she should change her entire wardrobe, hair, glasses, braces, and Betty still treats Amanda like she's not a terrible person. I don't know if you've noticed, but anytime Amanda is insulting Betty, she's still standing uncomfortably close to her, because Amanda kind of wants to be near her. I think America has done such a great job of balancing the sort of fun, quirky physical comedy while keeping the character very real and grounded. We all work around her.

Ruthie and the Beer Wench: When I see the script and I get to play someone other than Amanda [like Ruthie, the assistant at Sofia's magazine or the Beer Wench, from Amanda's acting reel], I call everyone I know. I make my grandmother swear to secrecy that she's not going to tell all her friends at church the plot of the upcoming episodes. I'm incredibly fortunate that I like to go there and just do crazy things. But honestly, I don't have a lot of dignity. (Laughs.) The writing is so great, because for all the crazy fun things I get to do that are over-the-top, every now and then, the writers make sure that Amanda stays kind of vulnerable. For every ten times she insults Betty, there's one time she might say something that's marginally nice.

The writers find a way to make sure we see that even these awful characters have souls.

Finding Daddy: It's a whole new side to the character, because as far as we knew, Amanda's parents didn't really like her. That's why she didn't go home for Thanksgiving and hung out with Marc in Wilhelmina's office instead. We didn't really think Amanda had any relationship with her parents, but finding out that her parents weren't who she thought they were is a whole different twist. It sets up a lot of comedy and drama because yes, it's very serious. A girl is trying to figure out where she

comes from. But it's also hysterical that Fey Sommers is her real mother, which you'd better believe gives Amanda a whole new sense of importance and entitlement.

I Heart Halston: Halston and I have become very close. Halston's actually a little doggie named Maggie, and I call her Maggle Rock after *Fraggle Rock*. Maggie doesn't have to do anything, and she's a comic genius. If there's a camera on Maggie's face, everyone starts laughing, so I have to work a lot harder. You know what they say about not working with kids and animals? Try an ugly dog with warts—there's no beating that dog.

Becki Newton wore a fat suit when her character, Amanda, spent the summer binge eating from stress.

MARC, AMANDA, and BETTY

Oh, we all know the besties get the best lines! (Thank goodness Betty is occasionally around to put them in their place.)

Amanda:
I think I'm gonna pass.

Marc:
You're not passing. I'm not going stag, hag.

Amanda:
You'll have to buy your own beer, queer.

Marc:
You can't just ditch, bi-

Amanda:
Oh, shut up!

Amanda:
Keep working—a little more overtime and you can switch to Invisaligns.

Marc:
When did catwalk become fatwalk?

Amanda:
Who cares about carbs when you're from Queens, right?

Amanda:
I can barely leave the house with an out-of-season handbag and you show up on a daily basis looking like a yard sale and don't care. It's like you were genetically engineered without the fear gene.

Amanda:
Have you been smoking one of your ponchos?

Betty:
Wait a minute—you need my help? The girl you've tormented for the last six months?

Marc:
I think "tormented" is a little severe.

Betty:
On my second day here, you got me to eat glue by telling me it was white chocolate. I could have died!

Marc:
I only let you eat two pieces.

Amanda:
Hi, you the "before?"

Betty:
Huh?

Amanda:
Before and after. The photo shoot.

Marc:
You must prove your loyalty to the Queen.

Amanda:
You?

Marc:
Wilhelmina!

Betty:
You keep walking by Daniel's office saying really loud that you have big plans tomorrow with this new guy you're seeing.

Amanda:
Not anymore. Jerk called an hour ago and says he has to spend the day with his wife and kids. I'm like, grow a pair, will you? I am so over men. They all suck.

Amanda:
But it's your mother. I'm the love of your life. Remember?

Marc:
You are officially released from beard duty. Consider yourself shaved.

Amanda:
Oh look. It's Scary Bradshaw and a side of potatoes.

"They don't make situations in the show so far-fetched that you can't understand how they could happen.

—Judith Light

Putting the Family in Business!
Claire Meade

Oh, Claire. She's the character on *Ugly Betty* who has the most relatable sorrows—her husband was a cheater, she was/is addicted to alcohol and landed in rehab, her son sort of died but not really because he was just in the process of surgically becoming her daughter, she landed in jail for murder and then promptly escaped to the Hamptons . . . oh, forget what we said about relatable. What's impressive about Claire, actually, is that she keeps her humanity through all her travails—she's stubborn and will fight for her family. Even if her family is full of lunatics.

For eight years, starting in 1984, Judith played Angela Bower on *Who's the Boss?* and she really doesn't mind too much if you start singing the theme song to her. (Michael Urie has done it and reported that she laughed.) Judith's work onstage has been as acclaimed as her performances on the small screen; she received the Helen Hayes Award for her performance in *Wit* as an academic struggling with cancer. Judith has been married to her husband, Robert Desiderio, for twenty-three years—they met on the set of *One Life to Live*.

A Conversation with Judith Light

The Meades' MO: [They] have all this money and a fabulous town house in New York. And they have fabulous clothes and incredible style, but . . . Claire's an alcoholic and her son is a drug addict. The only one who's healthy at all in the family is Alexis, the daughter, because she became who she wanted to be. But Claire and Bradford had a terrible relationship. It's like, God, you would think you'd want to be these people, but you don't want to be these people. You want to be in Betty's family.

Married Life: I was talking to Alan Dale [who plays Bradford Meade] about the relationship between our characters. I said, "Alan, you know what? If they don't love each other, none of this will matter." I said, "I just want you to know that I'm going to play this with the depth of love and passion that I have for you as my husband, as the father of my children, so that people will understand part of what's driving this woman." You begin to understand her in a way that you might not if she was just this

crazy, trying-to-recover alcoholic who was being put in rehab all the time.

Jailbird: They don't make situations in the show so far-fetched that you can't understand how they could happen. They just create a circumstance, like putting Claire in prison. Though by the time the last two shows had come out for the first season and I was still in that do-rag and that prison outfit, I think they had all had enough. (Laughs.) I think the reason that they got me into the Hamptons was: "Get her out of that outfit. Let the girl wear some makeup again!"

Wonderful Wilhelmina: Who doesn't want to get to say the things she says? We all wish we could tell people where to go or that they're assholes—excuse my language. She gets to do all of that! It's fantastic. It's like Donald Trump: "You're fired!"

Team Player: I've worked in lots of different places for a long time, and I've never experienced a coming together of so many perfect people for their jobs. It's almost as though it was planned that this certain group of people would meet and come together. All the wonderful producers, ABC, ABC Studios, the crew, and every single one of the actors, there's this incredible feeling that the show has been blessed in some way. I don't know how else to describe it, and I don't mean it to sound airy-fairy in any way. There is a substantive anchor of great love, respect, and affection that everyone has for everyone else on this show.

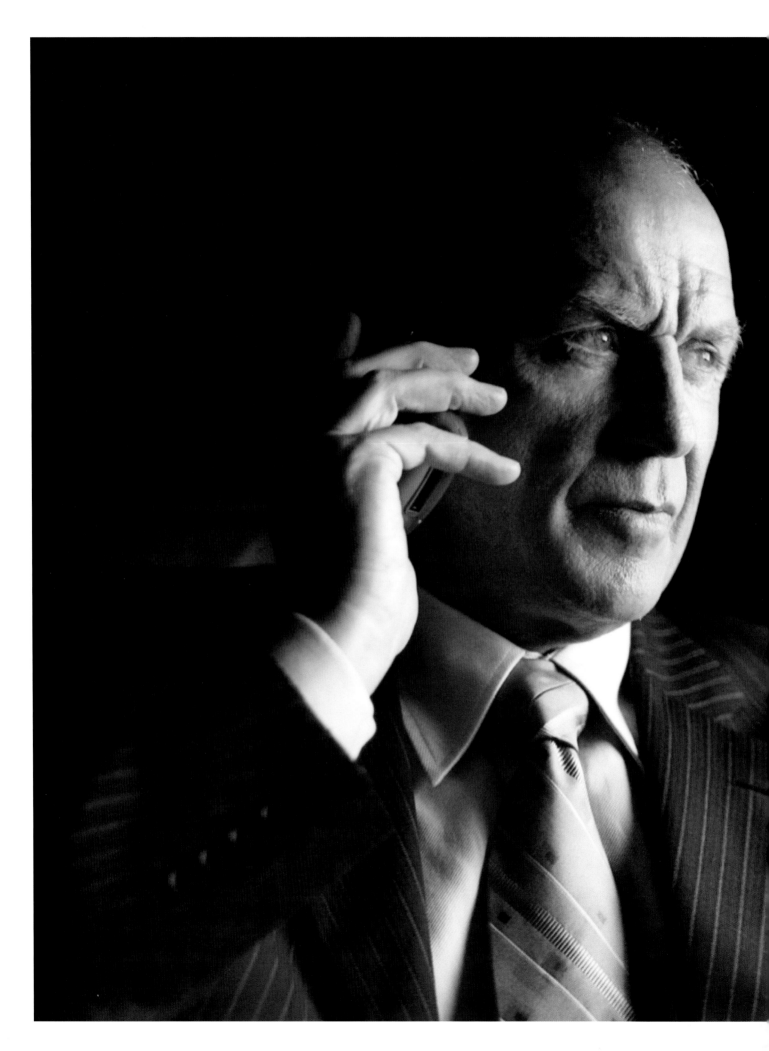

IN MEMORIAM

BRADFORD MEADE
1947–2007

Publishing tycoon Bradford Emerson Meade was pronounced dead at St. Gavan's Hospital after suffering a heart attack during his wedding ceremony to *Mode* creative director Wilhelmina Slater. It was a fitting end to a life lived in the spotlight, as Bradford—known as "Brad" in his younger, wilder days, as well as during an unfortunate midlife crisis about a year before—was a tabloid fixture as a result of the tremendous fortune he generated from his magazine empire, his tempestuous marriage to Claire Meade, and his twenty-year affair with *Mode* editor in chief Fey Sommers. Perhaps it's best to remember Bradford, however, for his contributions to humanity: his children, Daniel and Alexis, seem to have turned out all right—even though Alexis tried to kill him and Daniel inherited his taste for the ladies. The fate of his publishing empire remains in doubt, a fact that certainly drives Bradford's bride-not-to-be Wilhelmina Slater up a wall. The family requests that in lieu of flowers, donations be sent to the Claire Meade Legal Defense Fund.

IN MEMORIAM

FEY SOMMERS

UNKNOWN–2006

Mode editor in chief Fey Sommers was killed in a bizarre traffic accident, leaving behind only the charred remains of her license plate and a broken bit of her fantastic, face-framing Chanel sunglasses. Although decried by some as a "hoochie in a bob," Sommers was the defining personality behind *Mode*, causing a tremendous stir with her presence in the models-as-reindeer/Fey-as-Santa-with-music-box Christmas layout (see page 108) and generating naughty gossip with her in-office sex dungeon. (Oh, like you don't have one. Don't judge.) While her multiple-decade-long liaison with Bradford Meade earned headlines, the full array of her flirtations have yet to be revealed—there are persistent rumors of an affair gone awry with a young buck in the Studio 54 days. (Former assistant Wilhelmina Slater, then known as Wanda, won't dish the dirt.) Survivors include her beloved dog Halston and that receptionist girl at *Mode*.

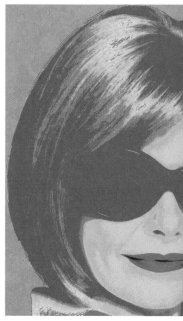

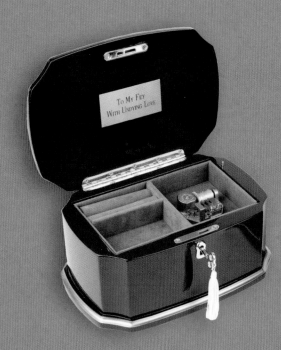

The music box, a gift from Bradford with a special compartment for secrets.

Does Your Office Have a Glass Ceiling?

Alexis Meade

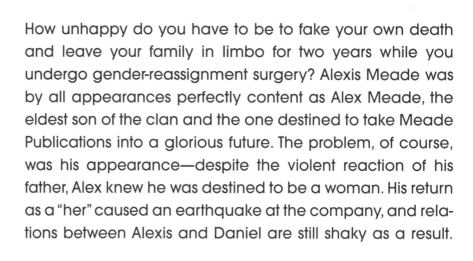

How unhappy do you have to be to fake your own death and leave your family in limbo for two years while you undergo gender-reassignment surgery? Alexis Meade was by all appearances perfectly content as Alex Meade, the eldest son of the clan and the one destined to take Meade Publications into a glorious future. The problem, of course, was his appearance—despite the violent reaction of his father, Alex knew he was destined to be a woman. His return as a "her" caused an earthquake at the company, and relations between Alexis and Daniel are still shaky as a result.

Hey, after doing the *X-Men* movies in full-body blue latex, playing a male-to-female transgender on *Ugly Betty* is no problem for Rebecca Romijn. It's a perfect next step for the career of the supermodel turned actress, who has proven her chops in both mediums. Rebecca gets praise for the insecurities she shows in Alexis—physically stunning, but emotionally stunted—a brave role in a society in which beauty is supposed to solve everything. During a backyard barbeque in summer 2007 attended by her *Ugly Betty* comrades, Rebecca was married to actor Jerry O'Connell—and was back at work the next day.

A Conversation with Rebecca Romijn

Betty Gets a . . . Friend?: I had been a huge, huge, huge fan of *Ugly Betty* before I met with the producers for the first time—and they knew that I was coming in as a fan. I said, "I just want to be a part of this show. You know, I would love to be Betty's friend! Betty needs a friend!" And they were like, "Well . . . we have a different idea." So then

they pitched the idea of Alexis, and at first, it just sounded like fun. I thought, Oooh, here's a character that hasn't existed in prime-time television before! And then I realized that it was a little bit more important than that—it's a pioneering type of character. It's a role that hasn't existed, and it's representing a group of people who haven't really found their voice in the mainstream consciousness yet.

A Big Change: Coming from the fashion world in real life, I have a few friends who are transgendered—a couple who are really close friends. But it's a sensitive subject. We don't really talk about it openly, but with any choice that I've made for Alexis, in the back of my mind, I never want to insult my friends. A lot of people keep asking me what it's like to play a man. First and foremost, I'm not playing a man. And my friends would be offended if I ever did that. Since I've taken this role on, I've met a lot of transgendered people who have come up to me out of the blue and introduced themselves and started telling me their stories. Those are the people I feel a

little bit freer in talking to, because they're open. I have met the most amazing people. Really, my research has come from personal experience.

The Big Twist: This season, I wake up with amnesia and I've forgotten that I've gone through the transition, so I've had to pretend to be a man who's walking in high heels for the first time or discovering boobs for the first time, which has been fun. I think Alexis is a very lonely character, and I'm hoping that she finds love on some level—somebody who's there for her, who's got her back. It's going to take a very special person.

Pals Off and On Set: The best part of this show is going to work and seeing your friends every day. We've become so close. You know, we've just poured blood, sweat, and tears into this, and we're proud of it. We're really excited to work with one another every day. It's always a treat.

Striking a Chord: Even before the Emmys, we were just thrilled that people responded the way they've responded to the show.

Rebecca Romijn's real-life husband, Jerry O'Connell, guest-starred on *Ugly Betty*.

When Alexis was Alex, he ran *Hudson* magazine, a Meade publication that covered men's fashion.

And you never know how these things are going to turn out. For whatever reason, the show has struck a chord. It's eye candy and it's gorgeous to look at and it's full of all these fabulous people, but then it always has a message. So at the end of the day, it feels like it's good for your soul.

Being Betty: I appreciate that Betty always maintains her honesty with herself and that she keeps it real. That's obviously the theme of the show.

Jimmy Choo Boo-Boos: I had to do about three or four scenes where I'm walking in heels for the first time. I return to the *Mode* offices walking in high heels, and I keep falling, and they wrote in all these pratfalls. I had my husband put on high heels for me. I said, "I need to know what a man looks like who doesn't know how to walk in high heels." He lasted literally half a minute. He said, "This is too painful. This is awful. I hate it." It was highly entertaining. I also did it for my own entertainment. (Laughs.)

In Style: Coming from the fashion world, I've always been really sensitive to scenes in movies and TV where they try and re-create a fashion shoot. I never feel like they get it right—except for this show. *Ugly Betty* is over-the-top and full of these outrageous characters—just like the fashion industry. There are people like Wilhelmina Slater in the fashion industry, and guess what? You have to grow a thick skin because of them.

A MODE GIFT IDEA

Marc helped create this photo album to convince amnesiac Alexis that she and Wilhelmina were best friends. Rewriting history is fun with Photoshop! In just a few easy steps, you can create your own scrapbook, filled with the kind of memories that you've always wanted.

We ruled the catwalk.

We had so much fun at the nightclub that night! You had to beat the men off with a stick.

We love love love shopping for shoes. Shoes and bags and other things that ladies shop for.

There was this time we sang karaoke. You sang "The Woman in Me." The crowd loved it.

Here are some tips for easy scrapbooking fun. Ask your assistant to go online and find some pictures of things that average people think are fun. Then, have him give those pictures to someone who knows Photoshop really well. Maybe someone in your art department.

Surfin' USA! Woo!
We love surfing.

One time, we went square dancing!
Oh what great fun we had.
Do si do!

Give the guy in your art department your photo and the photo of your friend (make sure you look fabulous!). He'll put your heads on the average people's bodies. Then ask your assistant to paste those pictures in a book and write captions. Vóila! You're on your way to complete magazine domination.

Work On What Counts!
Henry Grubstick

Name a TV show with a cult following: *Party of Five*? *Buffy the Vampire Slayer*? *Popular*? *Felicity*? *Jake 2.0*? Christopher Gorham has had roles in them all. The UCLA theater grad has played everything from doctors to superhuman computer technicians, and yet it's the part of lovably dorky accountant Henry Grubstick—the glasses; the sweater-vests; the Superman T-shirt on Halloween!—that has girls swooning. (Christopher says he doesn't get recognized as Henry on the street—it's amazing what those nerd accessories can do.) And sorry, ladies, he's married—to *Popular* costar Anel Lopez Gorham—and they have two kids.

Oh, Henry! The Clark Kent-ish cutie is Betty's perma-crush, an accountant for Meade Publishing who still manages to complicate her life despite his sweet personality. He's the textbook good guy—so of course he was going to give his relationship with Charlie another try, and of course he was going to do the right thing and try to be a good father to the baby. And of course he was going to pine for Betty the entire time, despite his stand-up nature. Will the star-crossed lovers ever make a go of it for real? It's something we just don't know.

A Conversation with Christopher Gorham

Will Henry and Betty Ever Get Together?: Well, the show is a soap opera, so they may. I don't know what's going to happen, but I imagine that it's one of those romantic relationships that will be dragged out for years and years and have many different formations. But that's great, because the fear is that if you get a couple like that together and then settle them, it's not as interesting.

Daniel and Betty: It's very much an American thing to fight against the boss and the secretary/assistant getting together—or, at least, for progressive American women who have a hard time with the whole beauty-and-the-beast idea of the prince who only realizes how great you are once you're pretty. But there is a big group of fans that really wants Daniel and Betty to be together at the end. And they fight. Henry-Betty fans and Daniel-Betty fans have online wars over who Betty should end up with. You should really check out these message boards. It's something else.

Regarding Henry: I had worked with Silvio Horta before, on a show called *Jake 2.0*, and so he called me out of the blue and asked if I'd come in, meet America, and play this part. It was going to be a three-episode arc. I came in and we got along great. It all happened really fast, so I didn't exactly know what I was going to be doing. In terms of Henry's look, I part his hair on the side like I used to in high school and make it very clean. The glasses we totally agreed on because I came in wanting to wear glasses. His walk—everything—just came organically, in finding who this guy was. I wanted him to have style without being stylish. He's put together. He does think about what he puts on. It's just not stylish.

Dress to Impress!
Christina McKinney

Christina McKinney is Betty's pal, ally, and confidante. She proves that there is human life at *Mode*, and, more important, reminds Betty that there is a life to be had outside *Mode*. She's the doyenne of The Closet, the magazine's stash of dresses, accessories, and shoes—oh, the pretty shoes!—used for photo shoots and bribery. But it's not all whiskey and crumpets for Christina—she hid a husband back in Scotland. Or, rather, *she* was hiding from her husband back in Scotland. And you thought those twiggy *Mode* girls had all the drama.

Good from the Get-Go: I had read a few scripts and it was a bit like, Now, which one was that? Was that the one about the people who are all in their thirties set in San Francisco or was that the one about the people who are all in their thirties set in Manhattan? I'd get them all confused, but *Ugly Betty* just stood out. The script for the pilot was so original and different. Silvio's writing was so colorful and so bright, even on the page.

Our Own Inner Betty: There's a little bit of Betty in all of us, really. We all bluster through the day, pretending that we don't trip up and fall or walk out of hotels with our skirts tucked into our pantyhose.

Fashion Plate: I've always been interested in fashion and creating things, and I would go through experimental stages. I had a pair of Dr. Martens boots, and I spray-painted them silver, then I put glue and glitter on them, and then I had tartan plaid laces in them. I thought these were the best shoes I ever had.

Yep, that's her real accent. Ashley Jensen does hail from Scotland—and although she originally auditioned for Christina using an American accent, the producers encouraged her to let it rip in her own brogue. A veteran of the small screen in the U.K., Ashley currently tag-teams her work on *Ugly Betty* with a starring role in Ricky Gervais's *Extras* on HBO. She was one of the three *Ugly Betty* actors to get married in 2007—her wedding to fellow actor Terence Beasley was held in Big Sur, California.

A Conversation with Ashley Jensen

From *Extras* to Regular: I had done a pro-

gram called *Extras* that was an HBO and BBC coproduction, and I was very fortunate that it was on the television over here—and I happened to be here. I had just recently got an agent and a manager in the U.S., and they had said, "Well, you're going to have to come out for pilot season now that we've signed you up." And I said, "Well, you're probably right." (Laughs.) So I came out and hit pilot season for the first time, which was like nothing I had ever done before. And it was all quite exciting and exhilarating but a little bit overwhelming. One of the three auditions that I had one day was this little gem of a script called *Ugly Betty*. It was like a little pearl among swine.

Wizard of Odds: On *Ugly Betty*, we've got our wicked witch and then we've got the flying monkeys. "I'm not one of your flying monkeys!" That was quite a good line of Christina's. I love *The Wizard of Oz* references. They're fantastic. So you've got your flying monkeys or evil step-sisters that are kind of like Marc and Amanda, and you have your Cinderellas and your Prince Charming. I think that Christina is a little bit of a twist on a fairy godmother. She means well, Christina does. But I'm not sure I know many fairy godmothers who say, "Piss off."

HIGH FASHION

V

FOUND: in Wilhelmina's office. What better way to show off a high-fashion women's magazine then by punctuating the space with sculptures of high-fashion women? It's all part of the master plan, production designer Mark Worthington says. "I wanted it to feel rounded. It is a women's magazine. I'm always looking at the realistic detail for inspiration."

TRUE PASSION

FOUND: in the Suarez kitchen. This piece is a collectible that celebrates Dia de los Muertos ("Day of the Dead"), a three-day Mexican holiday that occurs around Halloween and honors family members who have passed on. But it's not a morbid holiday—it's more of a celebration of cherished memories, and it's representative of the kind of spirit the Suarez household embodies. "We have people from all walks of life coming to the set all the time from L.A. and New York, and they're all, 'Oh! It's like I grew up here!' It's really sweet," Worthington says.

CHAPTER FOUR

FASH

HION

FOUND: in The Closet. This Gucci bag was the object of much lust within *Mode*. It's a perfect symbol of a young woman's attachment to nice things— Betty didn't love it because it was Gucci, she loved it because it reminded her of her mom. Marc, of course, loved it because he could use it to bribe *Mode* materialistas.

TRUE PASSION

FOUND: on Betty. Costume designer Patricia Field gave America Ferrera the "B" necklace to wear on the first day of shooting the pilot—and it has been Betty's signature piece ever since. It is broadly based on a "B" necklace that Anne Boleyn was said to have worn during her courtship with King Henry VIII of England. (And if you don't know how that turned out . . . ummm, we're not going to tell you. Pretty history! Pretty, non-violent history!) Patricia was also the designer who came up with the "Carrie" cursive necklace on HBO's *Sex and the City*. Coincidence? We think not.

Fashion | SHOPPING

Ugly Betty is a tale of two cities—actually, it's a tale of two worlds within the same city. Betty's home life in Queens is vibrant, comfortable, and lived-in: a place for crocheted blankets and goofy magnets on the refrigerator. By comparison, Betty's workplace at *Mode* in Manhattan is sleek, austere, opaque, modern, and freakishly dust-free. It's the exemplary work of the *Ugly Betty* crew that goes into these backdrops—as well as the carefully crafted costumes, hair, and makeup that give the denizens of both worlds pizzazz and sparkle. How do you get the look of your favorite characters? Want to be as to-die-for as Wilhelmina, as alluring as Alexis, or as appealing as Amanda? We've stolen some *Ugly Betty* style secrets and can't wait to share . . .

Shopping for *Betty*: A Conversation with Eduardo Castro

Ever look at Amanda's clothes and think, I want that! I wonder where they got it? Wonder no more. Multiple Emmy–nominated costume designer Eduardo Castro dishes on why Wilhelmina wears ivory, why Christina looks like an escapee from Fleetwood Mac—and where Betty gets those fantastic sweater-vests.

What are your inspirations for dressing Betty?
My inspiration comes mostly from graphic, bright patterns on all kinds of fabrics, be they silk or cotton or wool. Or if a piece of clothing is ready-made, I might be inspired by a certain way the garment is cut. For example, on Betty's skirts, I like the simplicity of a pencil style or the flow of a bias-cut swing style. But the fun colors are what inspire me the most!

Where do you shop to find the costumes for the show?
We shop everywhere from Rodeo Drive and Santee Alley in downtown Los Angeles to Neiman Marcus, Target, and vintage boutiques.

Do you spend more time fitting the actors or designing new items for them to wear?
Fitting time is at a premium, as the actors' schedules are very tricky to work around, especially America's, because she is literally in almost every scene, every day. Designing, on the other hand, is a constant. I'm always drawing, sketching, and draping.

How did you envision some of the signature color palettes for the characters?
I followed the lead of Patricia Field, who was the costume designer on the pilot, and elaborated on what she set up. You'll continue to see Wilhelmina in ivory, Betty in a riot of color, Hilda in something tight and sexy, and Christina in something bohemian and eccentric.

Eduardo Castro.

What's your theme when designing for Wilhelmina?

Absolutely the simplest and the richest is best for her. It's all in how well something is cut and featured. A lot of embellishment doesn't necessarily work for her. So with her, it's sleek and polished, a lot of silks and a lot of really fine fabrics. We try not to skimp on the quality of her pieces, so a beautiful silk suit in ivory, taupe, and champagne might be a good way to go.

Guys often fall into the trap of wearing the same old boring suit, but you manage to jazz it up for Daniel and Marc.

For Daniel, we try to feature more piqué lapels and, again, a simple color palette. He wears mostly gray and navy. He can do dark shirts, and we've done tone on tone a few times. His casual clothes are going to get a little more interesting—we found some things that we haven't been able to put on him because he hasn't been clubbing yet on the show. (Laughs.) But if he does, we have some nice velvet jackets that Dolce made. And we're just having a ball with Marc. His blazers for the new season are dark with white piping—I call it the kangaroo jacket. His belts make more of a statement than usual, and instead of having him wear one pair of shoes throughout the season, we're doing colored shoes for different outfits.

And it can't be too tough to dress a supermodel.

Yeah, Rebecca Romijn has an amazing body. We are making quite a few pieces for her because of script specifications, but they're always on the sexy side with her, and very body conscious.

How about the two very different working girls, Amanda and Hilda?

We're going to make Amanda more fashion-forward than she used to be. We're trying to move her away from just being the receptionist. Ana Ortiz, as Hilda, has an incredible body and always works the textures and the tight jeans, but we're going to put her in more skirts and dresses than she wore last year. And we're giving her more fun shoes!

So you think all of Betty's duds are duds? Think again! As it turns out, some of Betty's pieces have quite the fancy-pants designer pedigree! In the episode "Petra-Gate," Betty sported a 100 percent silk top with a bold print created by designer Tory Burch. In "Punch Out," she wore a frilly top created by none other than Dolce & Gabbana. And the wedges Betty wears as she skips through the halls at *Mode* after she flirts with Henry in "Fake Plastic Snow"? They're by Marc Jacobs. Looks like Betty snagged something more than a Gucci bag from The Closet!

Dress by
ROBERTO CAVALLI

"Those 'Buenos Dias' earrings and that baggy blouse are a threat to good taste, but not to me."
—Wilhelmina

WILHELMINA SLATER

Every Little Thing She Does Is Magic

Think fast—what's the most surprising thing you've seen on *Ugly Betty*? That's right! Wilhelmina in jeans! Thankfully, she's over that casual fling. Her glamorous professional suits, perfectly cut ball gowns, and immaculate accessories show class and sophistication. "You'll notice everything we do for her is extremely clean and very, very well tailored and cut," says *Ugly Betty* costume designer Eduardo Castro. "Vanessa is so small that she doesn't need a lot of design detail—it will eat her up. Rather than something with a lot of embroidery and ruffles, you do a good fit on a suit and it will look like a million bucks. A well-cut sheath is always great and simple, too." It's a look that could rule the world—but Wilhelmina has to conquer *Mode* first.

FROM THE OFFICE TO THE OPERA

Your schedule doesn't allow time to fuss. Focus on designs that transition perfectly throughout the day.

1 Trench coat by **ALAIA** | **2** Shoes by **STUART WEITZMAN** | **3** Two-piece suit by **VALENTINO** | **4** Shoes by **SERGIO ROSSI**

1

3

2

4

SIGNATURE PIECES

Find a look that you love, and riff on that theme with subtle accessories.

1 Shirtdress by **B. MICHAEL** | **2** Dress by **DOLCE & GABBANA** | **3** Necklace by **MARCIA MORRAN** | **4** Drop earrings with topaz

"This is *Mode*. We are not about normal. We're about aspirational."
—Wilhelmina

Dress and jacket by
B. MICHAEL

Suit by **ETRO** | tie by **BURBERRY**

"OK, first of all?
I don't think we
should follow the
postpartum-
depression piece
with a layout on
baby-doll dresses."
—Daniel

DANIEL MEADE

Every Girl's Crazy About a Sharp-Dressed Man

Sure, Daniel thought Cavalli was a pasta when he took over as editor in chief of *Mode*, but he's a fast learner. In a job that requires him to look professional and be professionally charming, he has learned that a well-fitting suit is as indispensable as accessories that show some personality. "What works for Daniel are the to-the-minute modern suits that Dolce & Gabbana has been coming up with," Eduardo says. "Occasionally he'll wear Gucci, and we ended up with a very good suit from Alexander McQueen for him. We have been doing single-button suits lately that are body conscious and more fashion savvy."

BEST FOOT FORWARD

In the business world, everything makes an impression—make your tailor your best friend!

1 Suit and tie by **DOLCE & GABBANA** | **2** Shirt by **RUFUS,** blazer by **OZWALD BOATENG** | **3** Shoes by **BRAVADOS**

GIRL POWER!

Don't be afraid to flaunt your feminine side—the skirt-and-heels combo is devastating and versatile.

1 Shoes by **MIU MIU** | **2** Sweater and skirt by **ROBERTO CAVALLI** | **3** Shoes by **PRADA** | **4** Dress by **YVES SAINT LAURENT**

"OK, let's just cut to it. They soften the jaw. Slim the nose. Lower the hairline. Shave the Adam's apple. Then there are the implants: cheeks, breasts, ass. I'll spare you the more graphic details. But just to put a rumor to rest, they don't save 'it' in a jar."
—Alexis

ALEXIS MEADE

Hot in the City

Alexis invested some serious assets in her assets—and now she's earned every right to show them off. Her sexy style is slim fitting but not inappropriate; she relishes the attention she gets when she wears sheer fabrics in gorgeous jewel tones. (Of course, she wishes she were as confident on the inside as she is on the outside—but that's a matter for real therapy, not retail therapy.) "What we're doing with Alexis is trying to find a very sultry, sexy quality that is also a little edgier design-wise," Eduardo says. "We're trying to move into a few Donna Karan pieces that are a little more interesting than just a skirt and a blouse—very luxurious and very shapely. They're knits and they tend to just flow over her body."

Custom-made jacket | vest by **J. LINDEBERG** | shirt by **ANTO** | tie by **PAUL SMITH**

"Word of advice. Be who you are. Wear what you want. Wear it, flair it, glare it. Just learn to run really fast." —Marc

MARC ST. JAMES

Everybody Have Fun Tonight

Be it a crazy pattern, a bold color, or a designer gown stolen from Wilhelmina, Marc lives it and loves it. He owns his style and knows that what works on him may not work on anyone else, ever—but the fact that he can make it fierce is all that matters.

His flair is fearless—you know the best part of his day is waking up in the morning and figuring out what to wear to work. (Make that the second best part of his day—basking in Wil's aura is first, of course.) "We try to keep Marc sophisticated, but he has that

comic edge to him," Eduardo says. "We're trying a few double-breasted piqué-lapel suits on him that are very dandyesque. We're going to try a few hats on him this season, and we're going to start accessorizing him more with belts. He makes it work."

THINK PINK! AND BLUE! AND PURPLE!

A solid-color vest adds fantastic contrast to an outré shirt.

1 Vintage ascot and shirt by **PRADA,** vest by **J. LINDEBERG** | **2** Shoes by **KENNETH COLE** | **3** Shirt by **DOLCE & GABBANA,** vest by **J. LINDEBERG,** tie by **BCBG** | **4** Shoes by **MARCO VICCI**

DISTINGUISH YOURSELF!

Gray doesn't have to be, well, gray, if you jazz it up with your own favorite items.

1 Shirt by **EMPORIO ARMANI**, skirt by **BALENCIAGA PARIS** | **2** Shoes by **BETSEY JOHNSON** | **3** Shirt by **MARIANO**, dress by **DOLCE & GABBANA**, tie by **J. LINDEBERG** | **4** Shoes by **JIMMY CHOO**

"Screw you.
It's couture!"
—Amanda

AMANDA TANEN (SOMMERS)

Don't You Forget About Me

So you're living on a receptionist's salary and your rich, dead mother only left you a stinky dog. What's a girl to do to remain fashion-forward? Beg, borrow, and steal to be in line when Christina cleans out The Closet!

"Amanda is interesting because now that she's Fey's daughter, we're going to go a little richer and more off-kilter," Eduardo says. She's going to move away from her sleek, tailored looks into something more playful and fun. "We're trying to move her away from being the receptionist to sort of the party girl of the group," he says. "She's the Paris Hilton who might come to work in a cocktail dress."

Top by **SCB** | jeans by **CANDELA**

"I didn't want to quit! They just stopped appreciating all this."
—Hilda

HILDA SUAREZ

Just Can't Get Enough

Why should Hilda be subtle when she can be divine? She knows that color is her best friend, and since she has the rockin' bod she might as well invest in jeans that make the most of it. And those jeans are coming from some high-end shops. "We're doing a little more Dolce & Gabbana on her, and some Roberto Cavalli. She's going to have fun with dresses and jackets and fur," says Eduardo. "You can push her and allow her to go to different places, and she doesn't mind when we overdo her." And while Eduardo is using more expensive designers on Hilda, he still makes sure that, true to character, her pieces are on the affordable end of the spectrum. "The clothes are a little more refined, and on camera, they just look great."

COLOR ME FANTASTIC!

Patterns set you apart, and all women need a pair (or two) of red shoes.

1 Shirt by **MARCIANO** | **2** Pants by **JUST CAVALLI** | **3** Shoes by **BEBE**
| **4** Shirt by **CACHE** | **5** Pants by **HALEY #258** | **6** Bracelet by **GUESS?**

PATTERN YOURSELF APART!

Plaids, polka dots, tartans, and stripes will make you stand out against a sea of basic black.

1 Custom shirt by **EDUARDO CASTRO** | **2** Custom skirt by **EDUARDO CASTRO** | **3** Shoes by **VIA SPIGA**

4 Custom shirt by **EDUARDO CASTRO**, vintage vest by **STEFANO RICCI** | **5** Custom skirt by **EDUARDO CASTRO**

Vintage dress by **PAUL BLANCO** | vintage vest by **HYPERBOLE COURREGES** PARIS

"You are an attractive, confident, intelligent business woman."
—Betty

BETTY SUAREZ

The Future's So Bright I Gotta Wear Shades

Sure, Betty's look is unique (Marc and Amanda would doubtless sneer that "it sure is special"), but she is the ultimate lesson on how to carry yourself with dignity no matter what you're wearing. Truth be told, some of her individual pieces are quite bold and more than a little charming. And don't think for a second that it's easier to dress Betty than the other characters. Just throw some discordant prints together, right? In fact, Betty takes extra thought because she is the centerpiece of almost every scene. "Her vests are always fun and quirky, and we try to keep them interesting," Eduardo says.

Shirt by **PINK TARTIN**
Vest by **LIBERTINE**
Skirt by **EDUARDO CASTRO**

BEE YOUR BEST

Although once in a while it's fun to step outside your norm and try on a new you.

1 Shirt by **JUST CAVALLI** | **2** Custom skirt by **EDUARDO CASTRO** | **3** Shoes by **STEVEN**
| **4 & 5** Custom costume by **EDUARDO CASTRO**

GET CAUGHT:

Walking and talking on the phone!

"Daniel, I'm narrowing it down. Listen, what do you think about sending some-thing—like flowers— before I knock on these women's doors? Wait, I'm getting beeped. Could be Tuesday, Wednesday, or Thursday."

—Betty

Never one to put dignity before duty, Betty scurries around Manhattan in her butterfly Halloween costume to track down at which lady friend's house Daniel left his watch last week.

▲ The carefully unkempt look is actually all business; he's the man-about-town with a mandate.

▼ OMG, hair farm! Don't turn yourself into Bouffantra.

▲ Fierce. The suit is career but not conservative, ivory but not vanilla.

Let's not skirt the subject: thirteen-year-old

JUSTIN SUAREZ

is the teenage Mr. Blackwell, an honor student of haute couture, a disciple of the divine. Here he dishes on the best and worst looks from *Ugly Betty*. Learn it, love it, live it!

▼ This is *not* the poncho trend that they were talking about in the *Mode* September 2006 issue.

▼ What does it say about the work of a beauty salon when its smocks are this abrasive?

▲ Perfection. I love lavender! The shirt adds pizzazz to the otherwise Wall Street-gray vest.

▼ If you're over the age of two, thou shalt not wear an appliquéd seasonal sweater.

▲ Outstanding. The straps, with their delicate ruching, draw the eyes toward the bust.

▼ Down with down coats! The Michelin Man is not a fashion icon!

▲ Sublime. The belt adds a feminine touch and helps hide any candy-snarfing tummy pooch.

Do you fret about what to pull out of your closet in the morning? Don't. Let the stars guide you! Special this month: The cosmos really does have something to say about your cosmetics. Find your best makeup colors below.

AQUARIUS (January 20–February 17): You love to stand out, so your fashion choices should make a statement. Play with colors, textures, prints, and patterns. Don't adhere to those boring notions of what matches—who wants to blend in, anyway? Make it memorable.
Colors: Bright, bold anything!

PISCES (February 18–March 20): You're a sensitive soul, and you can reflect that in your clothes. Always add a feminine detail to your outfits, be it a brooch, a lacy handkerchief, or a cute barrette. Think of what you would wear if Lord Byron called you up for a date.
Colors: Blues

ARIES (March 21–April 19): You want to be in charge—so go with the power suit! Forget those ghastly shoulder-padded looks of yore, because a modern, streamlined cut can still get across the message that you're the boss. Pair it with drop-dead heels and you can take on the world.
Colors: Red lipstick, baby!

TAURUS (April 20–May 19): You're thrifty, but you don't have to look cheap! Buy quality designer items on sale or hunt through vintage and secondhand stores for their best pieces. Don't forget that old Chanel is still Chanel. (And some would argue that it's better Chanel.)
Colors: Earth tones

GEMINI (May 20–June 20): Since you're always on the go, it's best to wear pieces that can transition from work to after-hours fun. Buy a sleek pair of jeans and wear them with a cute camisole and a smart-looking jacket. When the sun sets, the jacket comes off!
Colors: Greens

CANCER (June 21–July 22): You think that it's silly to chase the latest fad because it's so obvious that some classics never go out of style. An A-line black skirt, tailored white shirt, and pearls are fabulous, now and forever, and you know it.
Colors: Neutrals

HOROSCOPE!

LEO (July 23–August 22): If it's on the cover of the latest issue of *Mode*, you want it. You're the most fashion-forward of all the signs, willing to be adventurous as long as it's au courant. Get thee to Fashion Week to find out the latest and greatest, stat!
Colors: Magentas

VIRGO (August 23–September 21): You're a perfectionist, so you want a low-maintenance look that reaps big rewards. Search for one brand that you love and stick with it. In order to change up your look, invest in some kicky accessories. (Virgos love fun eyeglasses!)
Colors: Purples

LIBRA (September 22–October 22): The clotheshorses of the zodiac, Libras have packed closets because there are just so many fashions they find appealing. Instead of buying things and never wearing them, decide on some favorite items to wear often—and then splurge on all different kinds of shoes.
Colors: Pinks

SCORPIO (October 23–November 21): You should work your woman-of-mystery vibe with pieces that go against the grain, like striking hats, unique jewelry, and fantastic handbags. You can carry off couture like no one else.
Color: Black (Think Amy Winehouse, not Marilyn Manson.)

SAGITTARIUS (November 22–December 20): While your sporty nature would love to just run around in nothing but yoga pants and a tank, your bold side wants to make more of a fashion statement than that. Invest in form-fitting clothing with a formal cut and rock the business casual.
Colors: Dark blues

CAPRICORN (December 21–January 19): There is nothing wrong with wanting the best for yourself, dear Capricorn. Stop feeling like you have to shop the remainder pile! Invest in quality brands—they cost a little more because they're of higher quality. No more mom jeans!
Colors: Browns

CHAPTER FIVE

EPIS

ODE

GUIDE

PILOT

Written by Silvio Horta
Directed by Richard Shepard

THE BOX AND THE BUNNY

Written by Silvio Horta; Directed by Sheree Folkson

Can you believe that assistant? This is *Mode*, not *Dog Fancy*.

—Marc (dishing to Wilhelmina about new hire Betty)

And though my bunny and I are a little worse for wear . . . we're here. And we're staying.

—Betty

Betty Suarez leaves the familiar comforts of her home in Queens for outrageous *Mode* magazine, where she becomes the assistant to newly appointed editor in chief—and the tabloids' favorite playboy—Daniel Meade. But Betty is a part of a scheme by Daniel's father, Bradford, to keep his son on the straight and narrow. Afraid of another sexual-harassment suit and knowing that "ugly duckling" Betty won't tempt him, Bradford hires Betty for the job to curtail Daniel's skirt chasing. When creative director Wilhelmina Slater plots to boot Daniel from the masthead, Betty proves her mettle by saving the magazine's top advertiser—earning Daniel's loyalty for the long haul.

Looking the Part America Ferrera (Betty): "For the pilot, the director and producers weren't sure how to do the braces. Their solution was to make me get real braces. The director said, "Oh, you should get them a couple of weeks before we shoot so that the wounds can heal." Luckily, the orthodontist said that he had this amazing removable contraption, kind of like a retainer, and it looks pretty real."

Betty's work life and home life collide when she takes The Book—the prepublished proof of *Mode*—to Queens for safekeeping. Her neighbor Gina snatches The Book and holds it for ransom, setting up a race between scheming Wilhelmina and Betty to get The Book back and to the printer. When Betty realizes that Wilhelmina has inserted "un-retouched" photos of a prominent movie star to embarrass Daniel, Betty fears that both her job and her boss's reputation are at stake. When all seems lost, Betty convinces the movie star that she's beautiful as she is, "retouched" or not, and turns what seems like a loss for Daniel into a victory.

On Frenemies Ana Ortiz (Hilda): "Ava Gaudet was playing our neighbor Gina, and she couldn't have been more brilliant. I loved having that catfight. I've never gotten to do anything like that, to have the license to just act crazy, and really be committed to it and have fun with it. Ava has actually become a good friend."

QUEENS FOR A DAY

Written by Marco Pennette
Directed by Jim Hayman

> We missed you at the party last night. What happened? Sale at the ninety-nine-cent store?
>
> —Amanda

Feeling out of place at *Mode*, Betty undergoes a makeover thanks to Hilda—but when Wilhelmina derides Betty for her, uh, brazen new look, Betty's feelings are hurt. Embarrassed, she asks Daniel to take Amanda in her place to a meeting with an important photographer—and Amanda creates chaos when she tries to imitate Betty. Overcoming her crushed spirits, Betty realizes that how she looks has nothing to do with how well she can do her job. Wilhelmina also is stressed to impress as she prepares for an evening out with The Senator.

Speaking of Makeovers **Veronica Becker (story editor):** "I don't think anyone on our show has their own hair. Extensions are clipped in. So when you're sitting there at home wondering why you don't have hair like Amanda—that's why. They promised to make me some."

SWAG

Written by Jim Parriott
Directed by Tamra Davis

> At *Mode*, fashion is currency. I know that's hard for you to understand because you're so very much in debt.
>
> —Marc

Christina opens The Closet for freebies, causing a fashionista stampede. Amid all the gimme gimme gimme, big-hearted Betty is gifted a Gucci bag, but ultimately decides to sell it when Ignacio comes up short in paying for his heart medication. Betty's ex-boyfriend Walter sees Betty give up her treasured bag and buys her a fake as a replacement in an attempt to win back her heart.

Orderus Interruptus: "Swag" was originally intended to air as the fourth *Ugly Betty* episode, but the production schedule caused it to be moved to later in the season. Setting up the episode as a flashback was filmed later to keep the narrative flow. On the first-season DVD you can see it in the order it was intended!

FEY'S SLEIGH RIDE

Written by Sheila Lawrence
Directed by Tricia Brock

Did you just gesture at me when
you said "Kwanzaa?"

—Wilhelmina

Betty, Marc, and Amanda attend a networking event where someone leaks *Mode*'s top-secret Christmas photo shoot. Wilhelmina goes on a rampage trying to find the source of the spill. Daniel is keeping his own set of secrets—thanks to a music box, he learns more about his father's relationship with Fey and how it publicly embarrassed his mother, Claire. Simultaneously, Walter seeks Ignacio's advice about how to get Betty back as his girlfriend.

The Inside Lingo Becki Newton (Amanda): "The writers had Amanda say 'Bring it!' when Ignacio offered her flan, and one of my favorite things is that throughout the season, somehow, instead of saying, 'Hey, what's up?' the cast would just say 'Bring it!' to me. It has become part of the collective vernacular. I'm actually hoping to expand it worldwide. I went on *Good Morning America* the other day and I got Robin, the host, to say 'Bring it!' It was a wonderful professional accomplishment for me."

THE LYIN', THE WATCH, AND THE WARDROBE

Written by Donald Todd; Directed by Rodman Flender

That is absolutely the
cruelest thing I've ever seen.
Someone's getting a raise.

—Wilhelmina (on Marc dressing as Betty for Halloween)

Daniel forgets his watch at the house of one of his conquests and makes Betty, wearing a butterfly costume for Halloween, hunt it down. During the chase, she bonds with Henry from accounting but is confronted about the flirtation by Walter. Amanda wishes she had multiple men fighting over her—instead, her relationship with Daniel becomes ever more strained. Betty finally learns that her father's HMO troubles stem from a much bigger problem: he's an illegal immigrant.

What's in a Name?: Becki Newton's character, Amanda Tanen, is named after Silvio Horta's assistant, Brian Tanen. Henry Grubstick (Christopher Gorham) got his last name from script coordinator David Grubstick.

TRUST, LUST, AND MUST

Written by Cameron Litvack; Directed by Jamie Babbit

AFTER HOURS

Written by Dailyn Rodriguez
Directed by Jim Hayman

So this is it, huh? Looks like a gay version of *Star Trek*.

—Hilda (on her first visit to *Mode*)

Imagine working in a sweatshop and not even being proud of what you're making.

—Wilhelmina (on the—sniff!—mass-produced appeal of Beaumart)

Daniel falls for Sofia Reyes, the brainy and beautiful editor of *MYW (Modern Young Woman)*, a new Meade publication. Wilhelmina struggles with her attention-hungry teenage daughter. Hilda meets Leah, an attorney who promises to help with Ignacio's immigration problem, and the progress on his case forces Ignacio to reveal a long-held secret about his past in Mexico. Ignacio rescued Betty and Hilda's mom, Rosa, from her abusive first husband in a brutal fight, and left the man for dead. Ignacio never applied for citizenship because he feared that his past would come back to haunt him.

Real Fashion: Darling, everybody is just dying to be on Fashion TV! Each time the channel made an appearance in season one, there was a special guest star as Fashion TV host: Isaac Mizrahi, Kathy Griffin, Tim Gunn. Our favorite? Tim's perfect sarcasm as he blows a kiss to Karl Lagerfeld and then says, "Eighty with a ponytail? Brave."

Who says *Mode* is a nine-to-five kind of job? Daniel's obsession with Sofia grows, and their flirtations at work leave the building. At the same time, Wilhelmina must entertain Ted LeBeau of retail giant Beaumart, a prospective advertiser with a penchant for country-western bars. She swallows her pride and a few shots while entertaining him, but it's her struggle to connect with her daughter that impresses Ted the most. Across town, Betty is assigned to review a hotel by spending the night, and spoils Walter's plans for a big weekend in Atlantic City. When he surprises her at the hotel, she's afraid he won't fit in with the swank Manhattan crowd—but realizes that what she really needs to do is face her own worries about being an outsider.

Anything for a Sponsor **Vanessa Williams (Wilhelmina):** "I don't know where the heck that bar was that we shot Wilhelmina and Ted LeBeau in, somewhere off Sunset in East L.A. Yep, doing shots off a women's belly? That was a first for Wilhelmina . . . and for Vanessa Williams, so that was quite a shock."

FOUR THANKSGIVINGS AND A FUNERAL

Written by Marco Pennette; Directed by Sarah Pia Anderson

It's like I'm this close to splitting a Cobb salad with Sarah Jessica Parker and talking about shoes.

—Daniel (on waiting for Sofia to get in touch with him)

The holiday season brings a load of stress, as Daniel meets Sofia's too-good-to-be-true boyfriend, Hunter, and Marc and Amanda are caught playing dress-up at *Mode* and snooping around Wilhelmina's office. (Why did they think crank-calling the mysterious masked woman was a good idea? Why?) Betty tries to plan a nice Thanksgiving with her family—including Santos, who is trying to get back into Hilda's good graces—but Daniel keeps interrupting as he frets about how to impress Sofia and steal her away from hunky Hunter. The holiday at the Suarez home comes to an awkward end as Leah runs off with their money, leaving Hilda in the lurch and Ignacio without a lawyer.

Turkey Time: Wilhelmina isn't a Butterball-turkey-hotline kind of woman, of course—so who would she call for advice on preparing a Christmas turkey? Martha! Martha! Martha! *Betty* fan Martha Stewart guest-starred as Willie's go-to gal for giblet advice. (And broke the news to her about what giblets really are . . .)

LOSE THE BOSS

Written by Oliver Goldstick
Directed by Ken Whittingham

Back off, girlfriends! Stop pawin' my piece, 'less you gonna show me some benjies, know what I'm sayin'?

—Wilhelmina

With Daniel out of commission at the Suarez home with the mother of all hangovers, Betty steps in to arrange *Mode's* exclusive photo shoot of a celebrity baby. Without Daniel at *Mode*, Betty finds that nobody will listen to her—especially an overeager, "edgy" stylist who wants to dress the baby in chain-mail armor and douse it in water. Some time with the Suarez family teaches Daniel that not all families are like his own fractured clan, prompting him to tell Sofia that he's ready to settle down with her. Impressed, Sofia decides to have a real relationship with Daniel. Daniel's not the only one impressing Sofia, however: Betty's smarts in handling the baby fiasco prompt Sofia to offer Betty a job.

Wherefore Art Thou, Mustachio? Tony Plana (Ignacio): "I had been filming with directors on the set for several days with the mustache, and when the makeup folks took it off, the director said, 'That's not real?' They do an amazing job. When I first auditioned, I had a mustache, and Silvio liked it. It gives him kind of a working-class, very Latino look that I also like. You know, they say people with mustaches are wise."

FAKE PLASTIC SNOW

Written by Veronica Becker & Sarah Kucserka
Directed by Jim Hayman

SOFIA'S CHOICE

Written by Silvio Horta
Directed by Jim Hayman

It's about the party. I'm supposed to oversee the budget, so I guess I'll be on top of you for the next couple of days—party-wise.

—Henry

Ted took me to an outlet mall. I shopped next to fat people.

—Wilhelmina

Mode gets festive as Betty and Amanda plan the office Christmas party—and the spirit of the season seems to move lovable accountant Henry to, you know, make a move. A disastrous evening at Walter's Pro-Buy holiday party opens Betty's eyes to what a life with Walter might be like and makes Henry seem all the more appealing. Betty is also distracted by the job offer from Sofia, but Daniel encourages her to take it, and asks her to help in the search for a new assistant. Amanda applies in the hopes that her past with Daniel won't interfere with her career trajectory. Daniel prepares to propose to Sofia.

Snowing the System **Veronica Becker (story editor):** "Betty's carrying this big plastic bag of fake snow, and Henry walks into it and it explodes. Everyone said: 'We cannot do fake snow. It's too expensive.' And we're like: 'Well, maybe if we name the episode 'Fake Plastic Snow' they won't be able to not give us the fake snow.' We blocked out hours for the scene because if they had to do another take, they had to clean up all the snow. They did it once, and it was perfect."

Betty learns that too-good-to-be-true Hunter has a secret: he's actually Hunter No. 9 at the local strip club! It turns out that Sofia hired Hunter to pose as her boyfriend to make Daniel jealous, as part of her master scheme to get a killer cover story for her first *MYW* issue: "From Fling to Ring in Sixty Days." Betty rushes to tell Daniel the truth, but it's too late: Sofia stuns Daniel on live TV, revealing that their engagement is a sham and making a fool out of him. Ever honorable, Betty quits her new job at *MYW* in disgust. Another heart is broken when Ted dumps Wilhelmina, but thankfully she returns to her gloriously bitchy ways.

Doggone Lust **Eric Mabius (Daniel):** "I always get the comment, 'Wow, I can't imagine getting to go to work and having to pretend to sleep with Salma Hayek.' Salma's taken in quite a few stray dogs over the years, and she has a menagerie in tow. On any given day on set, she would have two or three of those stray dogs around here. Between takes, I say, 'Those dogs jumping on top of you are really making me feel extra sexy.' (Laughs.)"

IN OR OUT

Written by Myra Jo Martino
Directed by Michael Spiller

DANIEL:

"Fashion Week." Five months ago you thought Cavalli was a pasta.

BETTY:

So did you.

Aha, it's the revenge of Willie! As Daniel hides out after his heartbreak, Wilhelmina puts her *Mode* takeover plan into action, making a list of who will be fired in her new regime. Marc is dismayed to find that Amanda is on Wilhelmina's "out" list. Betty tries to raise Daniel's spirits by setting him up on a date, but Amanda—with an eye on impressing Wilhelmina—sabotages the date. Betty arrives in time to hide the fact he's been stood up, and Daniel confesses that he misses his dead big brother, Alex. Wilhelmina visits her friend the Masked Woman, who takes the bandages off and is revealed to be Alex—now Alexis—Meade, new and improved after gender-reassignment surgery.

Good Sport **Marco Pennette (executive producer):** "We talked about Alexis as a transgendered person, and Rebecca Romijn was coming in for a meeting, and everyone said, 'It would be amazing if she agreed to do this.' We're all sitting in the writers' room waiting to hear her slap someone. And we were floored: she was totally game. That was the day I fell in love with Rebecca Romijn."

I'M COMING OUT

Written by James Parriott
Directed by Wendey Stanzler

What Mr. Meade doesn't know is that while he may have lost a son, he gained a daughter. Hi, Daddy. I'm back.

—Alexis

Not afraid of making a splash, Alexis Meade debuts her new look at New York Fashion Week—incidentally, the most important time of year for *Mode*. Daniel and Becks engage in their yearly bet—one dollar to the man who lands the hottest model at Fashion Week. They both set their sites on statuesque and stunning Alexis. Hilda, freshly out of a job, comes to Fashion Week to work as a temp. Betty is angry when Hilda steals her thunder, time and time again, but Daniel's got bigger sister issues when Alex/Alexis announces to the entire crowd that she's back and that she's had a sex change. Not only that, she has also supplied new evidence leading to Bradford's arrest for the murder of Fey Sommers.

I Got My Eyes on You **Vanessa Williams (Wilhelmina):** "When Wilhelmina wakes up the day after the Doctor Wong treatment and her eyes are swollen shut—those are prosthetics! My neck actually hurt after shooting that day because they had pieces of plastic on my eyelids. I had to kill my neck to look under them all day. But it was a brilliant job, makeup wise."

BROTHERS

Written by Shelia Lawrence
Directed by Lev L. Spiro

It's like Cain and Abel.
If Abel was a woman.
Who used to be a man.

—Betty

DERAILED

Written by Cameron Litvack
Directed by Jim Hayman

You may be new at being
a woman, but you're an old pro
at being a bitch!

—Wilhelmina

It's the aftermath of Alexis's return, and there's a power play at *Mode*. With Bradford in the clink, Alexis fires Daniel and names Wilhelmina editor in chief. Daniel challenges the legality of this action, and Daniel and Alexis end up bickering like children. Betty tries to avoid Walter by taking Claire to a spa and, in a confessional moment, tells Claire that she's staying with Walter because of advice from her mother: hang on to love no matter what. Claire tells Betty that her mother only would have wanted to see her happy, leading Betty to realize that she has to dump Walter because her heart belongs to Henry. Before Betty can reveal her feelings, Henry's ex-girlfriend Charlie comes to town to try and work things out.

Neighborly Support Judith Light (Claire): "You know how in New York, there are thin walls in between the apartments? The people who were sitting in the next apartment to my friend's were watching *Ugly Betty*, too, and when I said, 'I killed Fey Sommers,' they screamed 'NOOOO!!!' It was hysterical."

Frenemies are created right and left: Betty meets a lovely girl in the *Mode* cafeteria—she's new to New York and a little overwhelmed. Betty's initial impression is crushed when her new pal turns out to be Henry's girlfriend, Charlie. Betty confesses to Henry that she has a crush on him, and that she broke up with Walter for him, but Henry, newly committed to Charlie, bemoans the timing of it all. The blizzard shuts down the subway system, stranding Santos, Justin, and Hilda on the train. Upset that they're going to miss the opening of *Hairspray*, Justin begins to perform the musical as a one-man show. When a disrespectful subway rider makes fun of Justin, Santos stands up for him—earning Santos a permanent place back in Hilda's heart.

Subway Solo Marco Pennette (executive producer): "I'm a *Hairspray* groupie, and Marisa Winokur, who played the title role on Broadway, is a good friend of mine. I did that as kind of a little shout-out to her, and I told her to watch the episode."

ICING ON THE CAKE

Written by Dailyn Rodriguez
Directed by Jeff Melman

> Promise me you won't make the same mistake I did, Betty. Don't ever lose your dignity over a man.
>
> —Claire

Jealousy comes in forms big and small as Betty takes her orthodontist, Dr. Farkas, as a date to Charlie's birthday party to irk Henry. Betty's friends and family assume that the orthodontist is the famous Henry, prompting Farkas to realize where Betty's heart truly lies. Daniel tries to use sex to distract lawyer Grace from talking to Claire—who's confessing her guilt left and right. Grace catches on, but it may be too late when Claire turns herself in to authorities for the murder of Fey Sommers. Ignacio realizes his immigration caseworker, Constance, is taking more than a healthy interest in him and has to deal with her obsessive crush.

Crazy in Love **Tony Plana (Ignacio):** "I think one of the biggest surprises was the relationship with my case worker and the direction that went. I had a tremendous time. I was blessed by a wonderful actress, Octavia Spencer, and I just let her be funny. I just played the extremely worried straight man."

DON'T ASK, DON'T TELL

Written by Marco Pennette and Sarah Kucserka & Veronica Becker; Directed by Tricia Brock

> You never told your mother you're gay? Isn't it kind of . . . I mean, you're just so . . . sparkly.
>
> —Betty

Marc's mother comes to town, and Amanda, irritated at being dumped as Marc's fake girlfriend, sets up Betty to be his new fake girlfriend. Their fauxmance is put to the test when Marc's mom has dinner at Casa Suarez. Marc eventually comes out to his mother, who rejects him and leaves. Alexis wrests control of the magazine from her brother, puts herself on the cover, and races off with it to the printer. Daniel realizes that competitive Alex is now competitive Alexis—and that it seems he will always lose to his big sister. When Claire tells Wilhelmina that the only people who will ever control the magazine are Meades, Willie hatches a new plan.

Sing it, Sister **America Ferrera (Betty):** "We were constantly begging Patti LuPone to sing us songs when the camera wasn't rolling and to tell us stories about her amazing career. We embarrassed her—which is basically what we do to every guest star who comes on the show—but we did it by pulling up the YouTube video of her accepting her Tony."

PUNCH OUT

Written by Oliver Goldstick
Directed by Miguel Arteta

> Oh, look. Scary Bradshaw and
> a side of potatoes.
> —Amanda (on Christina and Betty's nightclub garb)

After encouragement from Christina to set some boundaries, Betty learns the hard way how to separate her work life and home life. Tabloid reporter Quincy Combs sniffs around *Mode* for scandal at the same time Daniel flirts with a model, only to find out she's underage and will go to the police unless Daniel puts her on the cover. Betty is hurt by her boss's disregard when she tries to warn him: Daniel yells at her to stay out of his personal life, embarrassing her in public. Adding to Betty's bad night, Christina confesses that her Fashion Week show came as a result of her helping Wilhelmina in her battle against Daniel. Wilhelmina takes another step toward marrying Bradford: she learns he has a foot fetish and enlists Marc to get tiny little fish to eat away the dead skin on her feet to give her the perfect pedicure.

Lovin' an Elevator: Be sure to check out the art that graces the back of the elevator at *Mode*. It changes every episode— and usually has something to do with the theme of that week's show.

PETRA-GATE

Written by Gabrielle Stanton & Harry Werksman
Directed by Paul Lazarus

> DANIEL:
> Nobody consulted me.
> ALEXIS:
> I think you were passed out under
> a pile of models that day.

Betty is in a funk. Still hurt by Daniel's words and Christina's betrayal, she calls in "sick" to stay home and pout. Hilda reminds Betty that she's hard on people who hurt her— reminding her of her best friend from high school, Trina De Paolo, whom she never forgave for ruining their "anti- prom" by getting a real date. Betty concedes that she holds people to a high standard and realizes that she should allow people to apologize. She returns to *Mode* in the nick of time. The underage model from the last episode? Not so underage, and Betty and Henry team up to clear Daniel's name from the con artist.

Down Under Demeanor Vanessa Williams (Wilhelmina): "Alan Dale is so different from Bradford. People don't real- ize that he's a clown. He's from New Zealand, so he's got this really big, thick accent. He's a man's man, but a delight and always smiling and cracking jokes and being a little bit naughty. He drives a convertible, with his dog next to him! He's a surfer! He is so not Bradford, who is very contained and very corporate."

SECRETARIES DAY

Written by Henry Alonso Myers
Directed by Victor Nelli Jr.

If this is what it takes to help my father, then I'll ride that giant robot horse all the way to Mexico!

—Betty

Oh, what's a little embarrassment among co-workers? *Mode* hosts its annual assistants' bash at Middle Ages, where Betty is determined to conquer a mechanical horse and win a huge cash prize—after all, tickets to Mexico are expensive, and Ignacio needs to go back there in order to re-enter the country legally. While at Middle Ages, Henry defends Betty's honor from Alexis's fratty assistant, Nick Pepper. The event forces Amanda to face her unsavory past as—gasp!—an actress. Wilhelmina convinces Bradford that Claire's violence toward Fey was not a one-time thing and enlists Marc to beat her up and make it appear that Claire has a violent gang working for her outside the big house. With her new black eye, Wilhelmina makes Bradford concede that Claire is dangerous and that he intends to divorce her. Score one for Willie.

Slap Fight Michael Urie (Marc): "I love that I got to beat up Wilhelmina. Vanessa and I have a great relationship. When we're on set, we're goofy and silly. I think without that, you wouldn't see our chemistry on screen."

A TREE GROWS IN GUADALAJARA

Written by Tracy Poust & Jon Kinnally; Directed by Lev L. Spiro

COUSIN CLARA:
Look at you—you're so skinny!
BETTY:
You're the third person who's told me that. Oh, my God, I love it here.

The Suarez clan returns to Mexico to help Ignacio get a visa, and the visit has many unexpected revelations. Betty learns more about her family tree after a mysterious old woman tells her she has a vision of "a tree with missing branches." The clues lead Betty to the home of her grandmother—Rosa's mom—who Betty didn't realize was alive. It turns out, Betty's grandmother never approved of her daughter fleeing Mexico with Ignacio, but now on her deathbed she wishes she could tell Rosa that she'd made a mistake. "Fight for love no matter what," she tells Betty, who can't wait to get home to fight for Henry.

Buenos Dias: It's the first appearance of Betty's "Buenos Dias" earrings! Trying to show off her kinda-sorta-not-quite bilingual skills, Betty wears a pair of dangly earrings in this episode that say "Buenos" on one and "Dias" on the other. Flash forward to season two, and Betty loses one of the earrings at Wilhelmina's pad when she's spying on her under the bed. Willie's reaction? "I smell a burrito."

EAST SIDE STORY

Written by Silvio Horta & Marco Pennette
Directed by Jim Hayman

HOW BETTY GOT HER GRIEVE BACK

Written by Silvio Horta & Marco Pennette; Directed by Jim Hayman

You are such a chick flick—
I would totally pay
twelve dollars to see you.

—Diane (Betty's dental hygienist)

Meet me at the Bow Bridge in
Central Park tonight at eight.
I'll be dressed as a nun. Or a cat. I
haven't decided yet.

—Claire

It's an epic cliffhanger for all our favorites. Claire breaks out of prison, Daniel and Alexis are in a car accident, and Bradford and Wilhelmina become engaged. At *Mode*, Amanda accidentally reveals the secret of Fey's love dungeon to Christina, and the duo is inadvertently locked inside. While snooping around, Amanda discovers a birth certificate indicating that Fey was her mother; Christina, in turn, confesses she ran away from her husband in Scotland. Betty and Henry prepare for their first date together, but the evening is spoiled when Charlie shows up to declare she's pregnant and moving back to Tucson. Henry, who was raised without a father, does the honorable thing and decides to return to Arizona with her. Meanwhile, Betty finds out from a chatty dental assistant that Charlie was two-timing Henry with Dr. Farkas—and the baby may not be his. And most heartbreaking, Santos is shot while at a convenience store and Betty must give the devastating news to Hilda.

Star Power: In addition to Kristin Chenoweth's role as Diane, the solicitous dental hygienist, this episode features Angélica Vale—who played the title role of Leti in *La Fea Más Bella*.

The second season picks up three weeks after the tumultuous events of the finale. With her father stuck in Mexico and Hilda grieving over Santos, Betty struggles to keep the Suarezes afloat. At *Mode*, Wilhelmina makes a power play as Daniel recovers in a wheelchair after the car accident and Alexis awakens from a coma with memory loss. Claire is on the run in the Hamptons and realizes that to get her life back, she has to bribe Wilhelmina to leave Bradford. Daniel helps Betty perform a ceremony to try to put Henry in the past, while Justin and Hilda learn how to say good-bye to Santos.

Eye Patch Ordeal **America Ferrera (Betty):** "A big part of this episode is that I slam my eye and have to go to the emergency room, and I wear a patch for the rest of the episode. So when we were filming the pratfall, I slammed into the glass and bruised the wrong eye—the one that the eye patch wasn't supposed to cover!"

FAMILY/AFFAIR

Written by Bill Wrubel
Directed by Victor Nelli Jr.

Betty:
Oh God, Henry. Have you been drinking?
Henry:
Yes, I have. But I had a glass of milk first to coat my stomach.

In an attempt to consolidate her control over the magazine, Willie takes The Book to her apartment. Betty, walking on the wild side, enlists Christina to help her break in and get it back—and they catch Wilhelmina in a compromising position with her bodyguard, Dwayne. Wilhelmina makes Betty an offer she can't refuse: She'll pull strings with The Senator to get Ignacio back to the United States. Amanda inherits Fey's ugly dog but comes to love him for the connection he represents to her mother. Christina tells Henry that Charlie's baby may not be his, leading Henry to profess his love for Betty.

Betty the Woman **Jim Hayman (executive producer):** "[In the second season] we really see Betty's growth as a person. She is still the naïve pie-in-the-sky optimist from Queens with off-center capabilities, but she starts to believe in herself and grow as a young woman, both in her relationships and in the way she decides that she's becoming a person at *Mode* she doesn't want to be."

BETTY'S WAIT PROBLEM

Written by Tracy Poust & Jon Kinnally; Directed by Tricia Brock

Christina:
Am I sewing an endangered species
Wilhelmina:
If you really want to feel bad, I have a hat made of bald eagle.

Betty and Henry bemoan the terrible timing of their relationship woes and agree to wait until the paternity of the baby is determined before they officially date. Unfortunately for Henry, there's a new man in town: Gio, *Mode*'s ambitious sandwich guy, bonds with Betty and encourages her to follow her dream of becoming a writer. After unintentionally getting him fired, Betty invites Gio on a road trip to New Jersey to get a fancy wheelchair for Daniel—but Justin discovers that Daniel can walk and is just using the wheelchair to gain sympathy from his hot physical therapist. Wilhelmina's in a tizzy over *Mode*'s annual Black and White Ball, where Marc and Amanda plot to steal the show by having Amanda get in touch with her inner Fey. After a brush with danger, Ignacio manages to return from Mexico.

Daniel and Justin **Eric Mabius (Daniel):** "I think this episode is the first glimpse we get of Daniel really doing something for others. Mentoring Justin has probably never entered his mind, but the scenes between us are really touching. It's sweet that Justin looks up to him."

GRIN AND BEAR IT

Written by Sarah Kucserka & Veronica Becker
Directed by Tucker Gates

A LEAGUE OF THEIR OWN

Written by Sheila Lawrence; Directed by Wendey Stanzler

Yeah, he's mean. Like Simon Cowell, but with a Pulitzer. My story can't just be Jordin Sparks good. It has to be Kelly Clarkson "Miss Independent" good.

—Betty

I know you'll leave in five months. I know everyone will say it's a mistake. I know I'll get my heart broken. But maybe it's worth it.

—Betty

Urged on by Gio, Betty enrolls in a writing class taught by the imposing Professor Barrett, and in a moment of desperation to please him, passes off a woman's story of surviving a bear attack as her own. Daniel stands up to a bigoted advertiser who has problems with Alexis's transsexuality, while Alexis's faulty memory causes her to make an embarrassing gaffe in a staff meeting. Wilhelmina meets with the heads of the other Meade publications and decides there's no place like *Mode*, while Amanda, in her search for her father's identity, learns a secret about Wilhelmina—that she used to be Fey's mousy assistant, Wanda.

Broadway to *Betty* **Marco Pennette (executive producer):** "I saw Victor Garber doing *Sweeney Todd* years ago. I think theater actors are amazing, and we don't get enough of them out here in L.A. ABC has been terrific about supporting all the ones we've had as guests. *Playbill*'s website gets lots of hits for *Ugly Betty* news. (Laughs.)"

Desperate to put Henry out of her mind, Betty decides to give Internet dating a shot and meets up with a blind date at a bowling alley. Jealous, Henry follows her, only to be saddened when he sees Betty's date sneak out. After trying to be friends for a night, Henry and Betty decide to give their relationship another shot, even though it means inevitable heartbreak. At *Mode*, as advertisers pull out of the magazine, Alexis remembers her father's opposition to the gender-reassignment surgery and Wilhelmina figures out a way to make *Mode*'s financial crisis benefit her plan to start a competing magazine. Marc meets a friendly photographer to whom he's attracted against all odds. Justin starts rebelling in the wake of Santos's death, but Hilda is too wrapped up in a new friendship with three other widows she met to notice the trouble he's causing.

Young Love **Marco Pennette (executive producer):** "With Betty and Henry, we wanted to explore a romance with an expiration date. You jump in though you know your heart is going to be broken. But that's a twenty-three-year-old in love."

SOMETHING WICKED THIS WAY COMES

Written by Henry Alonso Myers; Directed by Victor Nelli Jr.

> You know the fashion world—
> very homophobic.
>
> —Marc, trying to avoid being seen in public with his
> new boyfriend

Finally, finally! Betty and Henry attend a performance of *Wicked* for their first real date—but after a series of snafus, they don't wind up seeing much of the show from the audience. Gio inconveniently attends the same performance with his little sister, while Daniel puts the moves on an older woman with a big advertising budget during the performance. Wilhelmina overdoes her starvation diet, can't fit into her wedding dress, and follows Betty's lead to pack on some pounds. Meanwhile, Marc plunges himself into work to avoid being seen in public with his new boyfriend, Cliff. Hilda reveals she's been fired from her first salon job and has been hiding where she has really been going to work.

Pop-u-lar: Eden Espinosa, Megan Hilty, and Kristoffer Cusick play Elphaba, Glinda, and Fiyero in the Los Angeles production of *Wicked*.

A NICE DAY FOR A POSH WEDDING

Written by Silvio Horta & Marco Pennette; Directed by Jim Hayman

> School? It's the countdown to
> the Bradelmina wedding! It's a
> national holiday. I don't even think
> there's mail today.
>
> —Justin

Ignacio forbids Betty from dating Henry, leading her to move out of the Suarez home and into Henry's apartment, where she threatens not to show up at Ignacio's naturalization ceremony. Henry, thankfully, shows her the error of her ways. The fashion world is in a tizzy and a half over Wilhelmina and Bradford's wedding, with maid of honor Victoria Beckham constantly upstaging the bride. Daniel belatedly learns of Wilhelmina's dalliances with Dwayne from Betty and fires Betty for keeping quiet for so long about the affair. When Daniel tells his father of Wilhelmina's infidelity, Bradford suffers a heart attack on the altar.

Seeing Stars: OK, tell the truth: Isn't that dowdy bridesmaid dress Wilhelmina sticks Victoria Beckham in the worst thing ever? Someone needs some Beckham 24/7 to snap out of it! Fashion designer Vera Wang also plays herself in this episode, while the role of bodyguard Dwayne is reprised by Rick Fox.

I SEE ME, I.C.U.

Written by Bill Wrubel
Directed by Rodman Flender

So apparently everyone knows about the big fancy sex room except for me. It's sophomore year all over again.

—Henry

...radford is admitted to the ICU, where his family and *Mode* ...ongregate, and Daniel, Alexis, and Wilhelmina get into a tus- ...e. Betty heads to *Mode* to clean out her desk and encounters ...eekend security guard L'Amanda, who also has a crush on ...enry. Reflecting on her year at the magazine, Betty has a crisis ...f conscience that the job has made her a worse person. Marc ...nd Wilhelmina hunt for Bradford's will at *Mode* and encounter ...enry and Betty, who are under orders to do the same from ...laire, who refuses to flee the country until she knows Daniel ...nd Alexis are provided for by his estate. Wilhelmina makes a ...st-ditch attempt to marry Bradford on his deathbed, but ...laire—the true love of his life—interrupts and gives herself up ...o the police so that she can say good-bye to dying Bradford.

...lo'Nique!: The comedienne and actress Mo'Nique guest stars ...n this episode as L'Amanda, *Mode*'s weekend security guard.

GIVING UP THE GHOST

Written by Charles Pratt Jr.
Directed by Gary Winick

If I've said it once, I've said it a thousand times. Nobody pushes Wilhelmina Slater into an open grave.

—Marc

At Bradford's funeral, Wilhelmina is doubly humiliated: she loses her job and is pushed into the grave. Whoopsie! In retaliation, Wilhelmina infects *Mode*'s computer system with a deadly virus, deep-sixing the issue just before it is due to ship. Meanwhile, she seeks funding from The Senator to start up a competing publication, *Slater*, with the best of *Mode*'s staffers, who bail on Daniel when Willie lures them with raises. Forced to put out the magazine in no time with a motley crew of loyal assistants, Daniel questions whether he is capable of such a huge task—but Betty encourages him to persevere and make his father proud. Alexis deals with a temperamental printer to get the magazine to press, and when a starlet in rehab screws up the cover, Daniel ingeniously decides on an all-black cover to mourn the passing of his father.

Behind-the-Scenes Tidbit: This was the first time Gary Winick directed an episode of *Ugly Betty*, but his feature work includes the movies *Charlotte's Web*, *13 Going on 30*, and *Tadpole*.

IN THE NEXT ISSUE OF

MODE

COVER STORY

A *Mode* exclusive: A very special sit-down interview with Justin Suarez on his heartfelt campaign to allow boys on the cheerleading squad.

LOVE!

What to do when two guys are making a move? We examine the love story of Betty Suarez, who must deal with her boyfriend Henry moving to Tucson. After he leaves, will Gio cop to having feelings for our girl?

CAREER!

Mode helps you lawyer up: We explore the legal options of Daniel and Alexis Meade after they learn that their dying father screwed up his deathbed video revealing which one should be the true heir to Meade Publications.

FAMILY!

When your sugar-daddy kicks it—turn to your real daddy! An in-depth look at Wilhelmina Slater and her rocky relationship with her father, The Senator. Also: Can your mom have a change of heart? Marc St. James and Mrs. Jean Weiner talk about the evolution of their relationship.

HEALTH!

The pros and cons of surrogate motherhood: We interview Christina McKinney, who agreed to carry Wilhelmina Slater's child in return for money to save her dying husband. Little did she know that the baby was conceived with Bradford's sperm as part of Slater's Machiavellian plan to take over *Mode*.

TRUE CRIME!

A Q&A with Claire Meade, on trial for the murder of Fey Sommers—her husband's notorious mistress. An in-depth look at what really drove Claire to insanity.

MUSIC!

Top Ten Ways to Tell If Daddy Is a Rock God by Amanda Tanen (Sommers)

SPORTS!

Is it OK to date your son's basketball coach? An opinion piece by Hilda Suarez

TV DINNER

This month, *Mode* looks at *Vidas de Fuego*

Are you like Amanda and don't speakey el Spanisho—and therefore have no idea what's going on in the telenovelas the Suarez clan always has on their TV? Never fear, here's a primer on *Vidas de Fuego*—yep, that translates to "Lives of Fire"—season one's tale-within-a-tale of greed, corruption, murder, and soccer-ball pregnancies.

Esmerelda—played by Salma Hayek in the first episode of *Ugly Betty*—is a maid in the home of the wealthy Mrs. Riviera. Esmerelda has the nerve—the nerve!—to try on some of Mrs. Riviera's clothes, and let's just say that Mrs. Riviera does not want maid germs on her couture. Mrs. Riviera slaps her, and Esmerelda slaps her right back. Hello, lawsuit!

Except! Seeking comfort, Esmerelda hooks up with Padre Pedro at the church, much to the chagrin of her twin sister, Eva. Esmerelda gets pregnant, and Eva—snooping around to find out who the father is, discovers that Padre Pedro isn't a priest—he's Ramon Castillo, wanted for murder!

Except! Padre Pedro says he committed the crime to help someone. Eva doesn't believe him and drowns her sorrows in the arms of local soccer player Galo—the son of Mrs. Riviera!

Except! Galo is also having an affair with his stepmother, Sofia. And Esmerelda is actually Eva, and she's not pregnant; she just has a soccer-ball tummy!

Except! Mrs. Riviera is poisoned with a glass of champagne! (Not a bad way to go, actually, when you think about it.) Will she go to the Fabulous Sample Sale in the Sky?

So who tried to kill Mrs. Riviera? Well . . . here's where real life gets in the way. The actors who portrayed the stars of the original telenovela—including reknowned Mexican telenovela performers Marlene Favela and Sebastian Rulli—weren't able to come back for a second run of six episodes. Day jobs, y'know? So the series ends on a cliffhanger. Ta-dah!

The masterminds behind this drama were story editors Veronica Becker and Sarah Kucserka, who sat down over a pitcher of beer and mapped out all the scandals before the start of the season. "We're always trying to keep a certain level of plausibility in our scripts for *Ugly Betty* because you want people to be able to relate, and things need to flow like they would normally happen in real life," Veronica says. "But when you're writing telenovelas, that goes out the window." Sarah agrees: "Very few people have been able to write about the person who carries the soccer ball around, the nun, the priest, and the club full of strippers and then have one of them pulling out a knife—and show it all in two minutes."

Photography:

All photography © 2007 American Broadcasting Companies, Inc., except: 4: Nicholas Cope; 7: ("Fey Sommers") courtesy of the *Ugly Betty* art department; 12: Selma Al-Faqih; 13: ©ABC/Adam Larkey; 17: Newsmakers/Getty/Newscom; 22-23: Nicholas Cope; 34: (Dr. Gabriel Farkas) Byron Purvis/AdMedia/Newscom; 35: (New York City) ©iStockphoto.com/Christopher Steer; 48: (top) ©iStockphoto.com, (bottom) Mark Coffey/©iStockphoto.com; 52: (middle and bottom rows) Nicholas Cope; 53: (top row) Nicholas Cope; 58-59: Nicholas Cope; 61: (from left) (phone) ©iStockphoto.com/Matjaz Boncina, (bagel) ©iStockphoto.com/Harris Shiffman, (carton) ©iStockphoto.com/Don Wilkie, (pink shoes) ©iStockphoto.com/Trevor Fisher, (rubber band ball) ©iStockphoto.com/Jill Fromer, (cork) ©iStockphoto.com/José Carlos Pires Pereira, (dental floss) ©iStockphoto.com/ Christine Balderas; 70: courtesy of the *Ugly Betty* art department; 72: ("Fey Sommers") courtesy of the *Ugly Betty* art department, ("Halston") ©iStockphoto.com/Eric Isselée; 86: (office items) Nicholas Cope (3); 87: (bottom row) Nicholas Cope (4); 98: ©iStockphoto.com/Eric Isselée; 106: Nicholas Cope; 107-109: courtesy of the *Ugly Betty* art department; 114: Nicholas Cope; 115: (left) © Rudy Sulgan/Corbis, (right) courtesy of the *Ugly Betty* art department; 116: (left) © Burke/Triolo Productions/Brand X/Corbis, (right) © Louis K. Meisel Gallery, Inc./Corbis; 117: (left) © Ted Streshinsky/Corbis, (right) © Purestock/SuperStock; 122-123: Nicholas Cope; 126-127: Nicholas Cope; 131-132: Nicholas Cope; 135-136: Nicholas Cope; 139-140: Nicholas Cope; 143-144: Nicholas Cope; 147: Nicholas Cope; 152: (makeup) Paul Tearle/Stockbyte/Getty Images 153: (makeup) Paul Tearle/Stockbyte/Getty Images, (brushes) ©iStockphoto.com/Ufuk Zivana; 176: courtesy of *Ugly Betty* art department; Inside back cover: © Image State.

Credits and Acknowledgments:

Melcher Media would like to thank the following people who helped us make the book: David Brown, Daniel del Valle, Lauren Nathan, Lia Ronnen, Jessi Rymill, Lindsey Stanberry, Betty Wong, and Megan Worman at Melcher Media; Zareen Jaffrey, Robert Miller, and Gretchen Young at Hyperion; and Nancy King, Mark Miller, Stephen Saito, Alex Tart, and Anna Wahrman.

Special thanks to everyone at ABC and ABC Studios, especially ABC's Melissa D. Harling and *Ugly Betty*'s Samantha Thomas, who expertly supervised this book.

We are grateful to the entire *Ugly Betty* cast, crew, and creative team for their help on this book. Special thanks to Robert Bernard, Alison Cole, Eduardo Castro, Jordan Macadangdang, Janel Montague, Jessica Replansky, Cindy Rosenthal, Lisa Schomas, Chikako Suzuki, and Mark Worthington.

Finally, a huge thanks to Brian Tanen, who knows *Betty* like a Suarez and can out-charm Daniel. We couldn't have made this book without your careful eye and razor-sharp wit.

This book was produced by MELCHER MEDIA, INC. • 124 West 13th Street • New York, NY 10011

Publisher: CHARLES MELCHER • *Associate Publisher:* BONNIE ELDON • *Editor in Chief:* DUNCAN BOCK • *Senior Editor and Project Manager:* HOLLY ROTHMAN • *Associate Editor:* SHOSHANA THALER • *Production Director:* KURT ANDREWS

Bios:

ANN DONAHUE is Senior Editor at *Billboard*. She lives in Los Angeles, and while writing this book she realized that she is 70% Amanda, 25% Betty, and 5% Justin.

PAUL KEPPLE is better known as HEADCASE DESIGN, an award-winning graphic design and illustrations studio based in Philadelphia. His work has been recognized by such publications as the *AIGA's 365* and *50 Books/50 Covers*, *American Illustration*, *Communication Arts*, *Graphis*, and *Print*.

Atlantic Attire